**Studies in Contempo **
Series Editors: T. G. Fraser and J. O. Springhall

Published
T. G. Fraser   *The Arab–Israeli Conflict*
Dennis B. Smith   *Japan since 1945: The Rise of an Economic Superpower*

JAPAN SINCE 1945

THE RISE OF AN ECONOMIC SUPERPOWER

DENNIS B. SMITH

St. Martin's Press   New York

St. Martin's Press, Scholarly and Reference Division, 175 Fifth Avenue, New York, N.Y. 10010

First published in the United States of America in 1995

Printed in Malaysia

ISBN 0–312–12758–8 (cloth)
ISBN 0–312–12760–X (paper)

Library of Congress Cataloging-in-Publication Data
Smith, Dennis B.
Japan since 1945 : the rise of an economic superpower / Dennis B. Smith.
p.   cm.
Includes bibliographical references (p.).
ISBN 0–312–12758–8 (cloth). — ISBN 0–312–12760–X (pbk.)
1. Japan—Economic conditions—1945–   2. Japan—Politics and government—1945–   I. Title.
HC462.9.S578   1995
330.952'04—dc20   95–2816
                                                              CIP

CONTENTS

Contents

vi

Contents

SERIES EDITORS' PREFACE

There are those, politicians among them, who feel that historians should not teach or write about contemporary events and people – many of whom are still living – because of the difficulty of treating such matters with historical perspective, that it is right to draw some distinction between the study of history and the study of current affairs. Proponents of this view seem to be unaware of the concept of contemporary history to which this series is devoted, that the history of the recent past can and should be written with a degree of objectivity. As memories of the Second World War recede, it is surely time to place in perspective the postwar history that has shaped all our lives, whether we were born in the 1940s or the 1970s.

Many countries – Britain, the United States and Germany among them – allow access to their public records under a thirty-year rule, opening up much of the postwar period to archival research. For more recent events, diaries, memoirs, and the investigations of newspapers and television, confirm the view of the famous historian Sir Lewis Namier that all secrets are in print provided you know where to look for them. Contemporary historians also have the opportunity, denied to historians of earlier periods, of interviewing participants in the events they are analysing. The problem facing the contemporary historian is, if anything, the embarrassment of riches.

In any case, the nature and extent of world changes since

the late 1980s have clearly signalled the need for concise discussion of major themes in post-1945 history. For many of us the difficult thing to grasp is how dramatically the world has changed over recent years: the collapse of the Soviet Union and Russian communism; the end of Soviet hegemony over eastern Europe; the unification of Germany; the end of the Cold War; America's sense of a 'new world order'; the pace of integration in the European Community; the disintegration of Yugoslavia; the Middle East peace settlement; the continuing economic strength of Japan. Writing in a structured and cogent way about these seismic changes is what makes contemporary history so challenging, and we hope that the end result will convey some of this excitement and interest to our readers.

The general objective of this series, written entirely by members of the School of History, Philosophy and Politics of the University of Ulster, is to offer concise and up-to-date treatments of postwar themes considered of historical and political significance, and to stimulate critical thought about the theoretical assumptions and conceptual apparatus underlying interpretation of the topics under discussion. The series should bring some of the central themes and problems confronting students and teachers of recent history, politics and international affairs into sharper focus than the textbook writer alone could provide. The blend required to write contemporary history that is both readable and easily understood but also accurate and scholarly is not easy to achieve, but we hope that this series will prove worthwhile for both students and teachers interested in world affairs since 1945.

University of Ulster   T. G. Fraser
                                                             J. O. Springhall

PREFACE

By 1990 Japan was a superpower, not perhaps in military and political terms but certainly economically. As the Soviet Union fell apart the Japanese economy became indisputably the second largest in the world. The Japanese had the highest per capita GNP of any OECD country; the five largest banks in the world were Japanese; the Tokyo Stock Exchange had grown into one of the major international markets; the world's three largest security houses (stockbrokers) were Japanese; Japan produced more iron, steel and more automobiles than the United States; no nation was ever owed so much from abroad.

The way in which Japan has been governed and the nature of the political system behind that government help are fundamental to understanding of the postwar period. Japan was a parliamentary democracy, although one party, the Liberal Democratic Party, had monopolised the central government since its creation in 1955; in fact, the conservative forerunners of the Liberal Democrats had provided Japan's governments since 1948. This unexampled degree of political stability has obviously been a key factor in postwar Japan's economic growth. The Liberal Democratic Party built close, almost symbiotic, relations with big business and the powerful civil service.

Postwar Japan's military policies have been much maligned by its allies, and particularly by the United States. The postwar constitution legally demilitarised Japan, although by 1950 the foundations of the postwar armed forces had been laid. Since then, Japan's defence expenditure has not risen significantly above 1 per cent of GNP, but given the size of Japan's national wealth, this 1 per cent has meant that the Japanese Self-Defence Forces (the legal name of the Japanese armed forces) are large and well equipped. Japan is not a military superpower, but it has become an important element in the Pacific and world strategic equation. The sophistication of Japanese technology has given Japan the potential to become a nuclear power.

Japan's enormous economic stature has stimulated great outside interest in the country. Japanese is spoken only in Japan, and interest in the language is a reasonable guide to that nation's importance to the outside world. When the author began to learn Japanese twenty-five years ago there was barely a handful of books on the language. A personal survey of a large bookshop in an English provincial city, done surreptitiously in the summer of 1994, revealed ten yards of bookshelf devoted to textbooks on Japanese. Statistically speaking at least, this explosion in the desire to learn Japanese, and about Japan, is more impressive than the economic miracle.

This book has been written in the belief that history provides an excellent introduction to a distant and relatively unfamiliar nation, its political, economic and social structures. It seeks to assist those who are either embarking on the study of Japan or who are anxious to add to their knowledge of that country. It attempts an historical overview of the processes by which postwar Japan was transformed into an economic power which impinges upon almost all of us. The principal focus is upon political and economic developments, although not to the exclusion of the social dimensions of the enormous changes which Japan has experienced since the Second World War. It is widely believed that Japan's economic growth, in particular, was an exclusively postwar phenomenon. In reality, this spectacular postwar economic growth had its roots in prewar Japan.

Historians are often accused to being obsessed with emphasising continuity. The author is willing to risk allegations of mania and no opportunity is lost to point up the influence of the past upon the present.

Most of this work was written between the summer of 1993 and the middle of 1994. As luck would have it, this was precisely the time when, after thirty-eight years, the Liberal Democrat Party lost its hold on power, whilst Japan's economy reached the depths of its worst postwar depression. These events shook to their cores many of the previous comfortable certainties of postwar Japan. The extent of the confusion that has enveloped Japanese politics can be gauged the fact that Japan is now (in the summer of 1994) threatened with the creation of a 'new-new party'. Prophesy is an enticing but dangerous pastime which wise historians do well to avoid. Suffice it to say that Japan will retain its importance in the modern world.

ACKNOWLEDGEMENTS

I am grateful to many in helping, directly and indirectly, in the production of this book. My colleagues in the Department of History at the University of Ulster tolerated endless conversations about and allusions to contemporary Japan. Dr John Springhall read and commented on the whole work, saving me from innumerable errors. Over the years I have had the great pleasure of teaching courses on the economies of Japan and of east Asia with Dr Walford Johnson of the Department of Banking and Commerce; his contribution to shaping and refining my ideas on Japan's economy and its place in the contemporary world has been quite invaluable. Tracey Weir, one of my research students, endured innumerable discussions about postwar Japanese politics and shared much of her knowledge of labyrinthine political manoeuvrings of the 1970s and 1980s; she also saved me from making one horrendous factual error. Gillian Coward was kind enough to produce the map of north-east Asia. Finally, a word of sincere gratitude to the generations of undergraduate students who have bravely ventured onto my courses on modern and contemporary Japan. Their questions, discussions, arguments, improbably even their essays and examination papers, have contributed more than they know to this work.

A NOTE ON CONVENTIONS

Japanese personal names are given according to normal practice in Japan, with the family name (surname) first.

Macrons (bars over 'o' and 'u' – ō and ū) are used to indicate that those vowels should be pronounced long.

A billion equals 1,000 million.

Japan and its neighbours

1

THE VITAL LEGACY OF THE PAST: JAPAN BEFORE 1945

At noon on 15 August 1945 those Japanese able to listen to the radio heard what is arguably the greatest understatement in history when the emperor of Japan declared that 'the war situation has gone not necessarily to our advantage'. This broadcast announced the unconditional surrender of Japan. It was the end result of six years of intermittent conflict in northern China followed by eight years of all-out war, initially with China and then with the United States and Britain. From the middle of 1942 Japan endured three years of almost unbroken defeat, climaxing in the Soviet declaration of war, which rendered Japan's military position untenable, and the dropping of atomic bombs on Hiroshima and Nagasaki. By 1945 many senior bureaucrats, influential politicians, elements in the army and especially in the navy, as well as the emperor himself, believed that surrender was the only viable option for Japan. This informal coalition, forged by Japan's catastrophic military predicament, was able to outmanoeuvre those diehard fanatics who contemplated a suicidal nationwide, *kamikaze* resistance against the Allies.

By the summer of 1945 Japan was at the nadir of its fortunes. The Japanese army was effectively defeated and the navy had all but ceased to exist. Strategic bombing had reduced acres of Japan's cities to ashes and production had dropped to a fraction of prewar and wartime levels. The country gave every appearance of having plunged into the

1

abyss of despair. There were no obvious intimations that in the half century after 1945 Japan would develop into the world's second largest economy, with a per capita income greater than that of the United States, or that the country would enjoy unusual levels of political and social stability. Contemporary observers would have been surprised by any prediction that Japan would achieve so much in the half-century following the Pacific War but, with the benefit of hindsight, it is clear that many of the essential ingredients vital to this postwar achievement existed in Japan before 1945.

Continuity and Modern Japanese History

In addition to 1945, there are two previous occasions in Japan's modern history when there seemed to be a decisive break with the past. However, in all three cases, there were vital lines of continuity running across these historical fissures. In 1600 the victory of the Tokugawa family and its allies ended a prolonged period of civil war. Under the Tokugawa shogunate, Japan enjoyed an unprecedented period of peace during which the economy became more sophisticated and more prosperous. The Tokugawa reversed earlier custom and isolated Japan almost completely from the outside world, although they did so to prevent collusion between their enemies and the foreigners rather than because of xenophobia. Many of the developments that took place in Tokugawa Japan can, however, be traced back to the period before 1600.

The second break came in 1868 with the Meiji restoration, a *coup d'état* that brought down the shogunate. This coup was the result of the tensions that had built up in Tokugawa Japan, and were brought to a head when the western powers battered down Japan's isolation between 1853 and 1865. The Meiji restoration proved to be the beginning of a thorough-going reform of much of Japanese life, but, as in 1600, there are strong threads of historical continuity;

the foundations of the successful modernisation of Meiji Japan after 1868 can be located in Tokugawa Japan. It is tempting to interpret the defeat and surrender of imperial Japan in 1945 as another seminal event marking a decisive break with the past. To do so would give a seriously distorted picture of the factors and forces at work in postwar Japan since it would ignore its debt to Japan before 1945.

Beginnings of Modern Japan

The Meiji restoration of January 1868 may not have been a total break with the past, but it tore down the Tokugawa shogunate and proved to be the beginning of a period of intense, indeed revolutionary, change. Within fifty years Japan was transformed from a quasi-feudal, technologically backward and militarily weak country into a major regional, and then world, power, and the foundations of modern Japan were laid. Fundamentally, this orgy of reform was a response to Japan's military weakness, which had become so clear after 1853. Japan had been quite unable effectively to resist the demands of the western powers and could not prevent their imposing the unequal treaties which made serious inroads into Japanese sovereignty. In the course of this transformation, Japan acquired the trappings of the modern state, many of the them based upon western models. The old, prescriptive and highly rigid social structures were swept away. Modern governmental and bureaucratic structures were quickly developed and a new legal system introduced. Japan built up powerful armed forces. A system of compulsory mass education was steadily put into place and by the beginning of the twentieth century virtually all Japanese children were receiving at least minimum levels of education.

Creating Japan's modern armed forces represented a social revolution. The introduction of conscription in 1873 ended the warrior (*samurai*) class's monopoly of the right to bear arms, and fatally damaged their claim to automatic

3

social dominance. Initially, the vital role of these new armed forces was to defend the new government from internal challenges, but they proved capable of beating China in 1894-5 and then, startlingly, they defeated tsarist Russia, one of the great European imperial powers, in 1904-5. At the turn of the century, a colonial empire was an important emblem of great power status. During the course of its military adventures, Japan acquired such an empire, obtaining Taiwan in 1895, Port Arthur and railway rights in south Manchuria in 1905 and Korea by annexation in 1910 (Lehmann, 1982).

Prewar Roots of the Postwar Economic Miracle

Central to the transformation of Meiji Japan was the creation of an industrial economy without which the spectacular economic growth of Japan after 1945 could not have taken place. In its turn, Meiji Japan's economic growth was heavily indebted to the development of the Tokugawa economy. Over two centuries of internal peace distinguished the Tokugawa period from previous Japanese history. In this tranquil environment, from the 1630s until the 1860s, the Japanese economy experienced unparalleled growth and structural change. Even before the Tokugawa established themselves, the economy had not been stagnant. Despite endemic civil war before 1600 the Japanese had developed one of the most efficient and productive traditional agricultural systems in Asia, and there had been significant development of handicraft industries, regional marketing networks, and expansion of towns and cities. The key to economic growth and structural change after 1600 was the system of control that the Tokugawa set up to curb the power of their rivals. The network of rules and obligations imposed on all sections of society, but especially upon *daimyō* (the feudal lords) and *samurai*, not only ensured peace but also in subtle ways stimulated rapid urbanisation. This urbanisation created concentrated markets for goods

4

and services, encouraging the commercialisation of agriculture and the development of networks and institutions to market this agricultural produce in the growing cities and towns. The economy became an increasingly complex mechanism, with large merchant houses buying and selling agricultural produce that the peasants grew for cash. The rural economy became more prosperous as many of the peasants diversified into the processing of their produce into goods in demand in the cities.

The pace and nature of economic development in Tokugawa Japan was greatly assisted by levels of education, another thread that runs through the fabric of Japan's economic development. The official ethical philosophy in Tokugawa Japan was a form of Confucianism, imported from China. One of the distinctive traits of Confucianism was reverence for education and learning, and this took root in Japan. There were also practical reasons for the spread of education and literacy. In the Tokugawa period the *samurai* became universally literate as their role changed from warrior to administrator. The merchants had to be both literate and numerate to conduct their expanding businesses. Education and literacy seeped down into artisan and peasant society; by the 1850s around 40 per cent of boys and 10 per cent of girls were being educated. Another facet of the Tokugawa economy which remained important both after 1868 and 1945 was the close involvement of the authorities in economic activity. The administration of Tokugawa Japan was dominated by the hereditary warrior class, the *samurai*. Tokugawa Japan was not a centralised state, and authority and power were divided between the shogun and a host of feudal aristocrats, the *daimyō*. Both shogun and *daimyō* became accustomed to interfering in and attempting to regulate economic activity and economic change. This official, pseudo-bureaucratic involvement in the economy would carry through into Meiji Japan and beyond. Essentially, the Meiji state inherited an economy accustomed to bureaucratic direction and based upon a relatively well-educated population with a prosperous agricultural sector and sophisticated distribution networks. It was an economy that had 'a potential for modern economic growth' (Macpherson, 1987).

As the leaders of Meiji Japan became familiar with the west, they realised that economic strength, and especially industrialisation, was fundamental to creating national power, and ensuring Japan's security. The new government put into place a number of policies intended to promote industrialisation. Most importantly, the government also set about creating a communications infrastructure, transforming and spreading education, establishing new legal codes and removing limitations on various segments of the population. The Meiji government had inherited a number of iron works, arsenals and shipyards which both the shogunate and some of the *daimyō* had introduced from the west. They added to this small industrial legacy by importing foreign technology and advisers, concentrating on strategic industries, but also importing textile and other machinery to act as models which, it was hoped, private enterprise would copy. The government tried to stimulate private investment both in creating industry and in building up the financial and other institutions necessary to sustain it. By 1880, however, the Meiji government had serious financial problems and the government was forced to sell off much of the fledgling industry that they had created to bale themselves out. The sell-offs of 1880–1 ended direct government involvement in a number of sectors in the emerging industrial economy, but formal and informal government and bureaucratic interference in the economy continued. The tradition of that involvement stretched beyond the Meiji period and into postwar Japan (Francks, 1992; Hunter, 1989).

Meiji Japan's industrialisation was the product of private investment and enterprise, although this private enterprise was vitally assisted by a variety of government actions. The powerhouse of prewar Japan's industrial development was the *zaibatsu*, the industrial and financial conglomerates that emerged, with government support, in the three decades following the Meiji restoration. Merchant houses had played

6

a vital role in the Tokugawa economy but they found it impossible to adjust to the new conditions and only one of them, Mitsui, survived to become one of the four original *zaibatsu*. The other three conglomerates to emerge, Mitsubishi, Sumitomo and Yasuda, were creations of the 1860s and 1870s. The founders of these companies often had close connections with the Meiji oligarchs who controlled the government, and benefited directly from government subsidies and the sell-off of government factories.

By the 1880s the *zaibatsu* were active in whole sectors of the economy, including railways, mining, shipbuilding, shipping, textiles, banking and insurance. The huge, multi-sector and multi-industry conglomerates that are a distinctive feature of Japan's economic structure have their origins in the Meiji-era *zaibatsu*. Between 1945 and 1948 the American occupiers fitfully tried to break up the *zaibatsu*, but they succeeded only in disrupting patterns of ownership and management, and this ultimately served to make the conglomerates more effective. In the 1930s the old conglomerates had been joined by the 'new *zaibatsu*' that sprang from the emergence of new industries. Since 1952 the *zaibatsu* have metamorphosed into the *keiretsu* which dominate the modern sectors of the contemporary economy.

The rate at which industry, and the modern sectors of the economy generally, grew in Meiji Japan should not be overstated. The economy only entered the stage of sustained modern economic growth at the time of the Russo-Japanese War in 1904–5; by then 15.5 per cent of the workforce was employed in some form of manufacturing industry. The textile industry was the largest element in the modern manufacturing sector, and Japan continued to depend on Europe and the United States for most specialist and sophisticated machinery and manufactured goods. The First World War injected a powerful stimulant into Japanese industrial development. The war cut off the flow of most European manufactured goods into Japan and into other parts of Asia. Japanese manufacturers took advantage of the vacuum in the supply of industrial goods to move into those

7

Asian markets that the European combatants had to leave. The demand for Japanese manufactured goods in these markets stimulated investment in manufacturing industry. Between 1915 and 1920, manufacturing grew at an average of 9.3 per cent, per annum, with metals increasing at 10.7 per cent and machinery and tool manufacture growing at 28.1 per cent per annum (Nakamura, 1987).

By 1920 the wartime boom was over. In some sense, the 1920s was a difficult, even grim, decade for Japan's economy as it sank into recession. This downturn was exacerbated by the catastrophic Kantō earthquake of 1923 and by a partial collapse of the banking system in 1927. Between 1910 and 1920 Japan's real net domestic product had grown by 61.5 per cent, but between 1920 and 1930 the rate of growth almost halved to 33.4 per cent. Throughout the decade Japan experienced deflation and serious balance of payments problems. Japanese companies had grown accustomed to continuous, though mild, inflation, and many found it difficult to adjust to deflation. Consequently, many small- and medium-sized companies experienced serious difficulties and there was an epidemic of bankruptcies (Patrick, 1971).

In retrospect, the 1920s was a key decade for Japan's economic development. Agriculture experienced severe difficulties but the manufacturing sector of the economy achieved a respectable growth rate of 7 per cent per year. During and after the First World War Japanese industry changed in a number of important ways. Firstly, there was a substantial change to electrical power, using newly developed hydroelectric plants which took advantage of Japanese geography. This trend had begun at the very end of the nineteenth century and by 1917 the horsepower generated by electric motors in Japan exceeded that generated by steam engines. The growing abundance of relatively cheap electrical power not only changed production methods in older-established industries but also stimulated the emergence of new ones, such as chemicals and, most notably, electrical machinery. New industries using high-technology

manufacturing methods emerged, including aircraft manufacture, which developed skills in airframe manufacture and
the use of advanced metal alloys, and the beginnings of
radio and electrical appliance manufacture (Nakamura,
1983). Laboratories that government, universities and
private companies set up in the 1920s to do research in electrical generation and telecommunications were the basis of
Japan's research and development expertise in computers
and information technology after the Second World War
(Fransmann, 1990).

In the years immediately following the First World War
Japan's economy increasingly exhibited that dual structure
which was to be a distinctive feature of its economy after
the Second World War. A dual structure is characteristic of
an economy that is in the process of industrialisation. On
the one hand companies emerge which are well capitalised,
are importing the best available foreign technology, which
have a demand for skilled workers and which consequently
pay these workers high wages. On the other hand, small-
and medium-sized enterprises appear. These do not have
access to large injections of capital and therefore cannot
buy in the latest technology. Normally their role is subcontracting and supplying less sophisticated components to the
more advanced companies. Since the levels of skill they
require from their workers is less than in the advanced
sectors, the smaller companies pay lower wages and their
workers have poorer conditions than their counterparts in
the big concerns (Francks, 1992).

The catalyst for this development was the difficulties
which beset Japanese agriculture in the 1920s after the government switched from supporting agricultural prices to a
cheap food policy which was intended to appease the urban
population following serious riots over the high price of rice
in 1919. Troubles with agriculture prompted substantial
migration of labour from rural to urban Japan just as
growth in the more modern sectors of the urban economy
slowed down appreciably. This curtailed employment opportunities for the migrants in the modern industrial sectors

and they gravitated into the small scale, more traditional urban enterprises which operated on a much lower technological level than the modern sector and which paid lower wages (Nakamura, 1983). In the more usual pattern of modern industrial growth the dual structure withers as an ever-increasing proportion of the workforce become employed in large-scale enterprises, with a concomitant steady decline in the numbers of small enterprises. In twentieth-century Japan, however, this pattern did not occur. The dual structure, in which the majority of workers were employed in small and medium companies, persisted into the 1990s.

Antecedents of Contemporary Japanese Management

In the 1910s and 1920s some of the most distinctive, and important, facets of Japanese management emerged, and these survived to become vital ingredients in postwar economic growth, although naturally with time they altered and were further refined. The historical and social background to Japan's management system is of key importance since 'no feature of an economy relates more closely to its social and historical context than the organization and management of its business enterprises' (Caves, 1976: 463). The key to this development was the former *samurai* class which was centrally involved in creating Japan's early industrial enterprises. The *samurai* ethos put heavy emphasis on public service, rationality and a faith in education. Just as the latter traits suited them well to serve as importers of foreign technology, the *samurai* zeal for public service led them to incorporate public welfare and officially voiced interests of the state in private business goals. The close and informal relations between business and government that mark present-day Japan have their origins in Tokugawa Japan and the earliest days of industrialisation (Caves and Uekusa, 1976). In the late 1910s and early 1920s many of the early manifestations of the Japanese employment system

10

can be detected as managers devised and implemented techniques aimed at retaining trained workers and also designed to head off growing political and social radicalism which began worrying the political and economic élites at the end of the First World War (Dore, 1973).

Economic Growth in the 1930s

The onset of the world depression in 1929–30 threatened to compound Japan's economic difficulties; in fact, the following decade proved to be a period of growth and significant change in Japan's economy. The 1930s was a decade of increasing militarisation in Japan, and the economy was tailored to serve Japan's war effort. This had a tremendous impact on the size and sophistication of the economy, important segments of which survived the Pacific War. Japan had been severely hit in 1929–30 but in 1931 Finance Minister Takahashi Korekiyo introduced a policy of reflating the economy through deficit budgeting, inaugurating a period of steady growth. In addition, the growing demand for goods and services from the military stimulated growth in manufacturing industry, both in production and in technology. By 1940, heavy industry contributed 59 per cent to manufacturing output, whilst textiles, which had been the mainspring of early Japanese industrialisation, made up only 17 per cent of the total. Building upon developments during and after the First World War, the technological sophistication of Japan's industrial sector grew rapidly. In addition, stimulated and often patronised by the military, new conglomerates grew up, most notably the company that would develop into Nissan after the Second World War. These 'new zaibatsu' challenged the easy dominance of the economy which the original zaibatsu had enjoyed, and indeed expanded, in the 1920s. The basic flaw in the economy in the 1930s, however, was that it took place increasingly upon the back of military expansionism, an expansionism that came to suck a rapidly expanding share of the national budget into the military after 1937, and which would, ultimately, bring something close to economic ruin upon Japan.

Change and Continuity in Japan's Social Structure

During the Tokugawa period, Japanese society became rigidly stratified. The *samurai* class were placed at the top of a tightly controlled social pyramid. Below them, in order, were the peasants, the artisans and the merchants. Legal codes specified all aspects of status and behaviour within each class, even down to what each might wear. Mobility between the classes was minimal. Economic development in the two centuries before 1850 profoundly altered the material balance between the classes, with the *samurai* becoming poorer and the despised merchant class and the peasantry and artisans growing more wealthy, but this did not lead to any significant changes in the structure of social relationships; until the Meiji Restoration the *samurai* retained their position as the hereditary leaders of society.

The Meiji government rapidly removed formal social restrictions on the Japanese, and particularly on men, but this did not immediately lead to anything like a social revolution. Politics, economics and society after 1868 were dominated by pre-restoration élite social groups. All of Japan's prime ministers before 1945 came from former *samurai* families. Likewise, the vast majority of the new entrepreneurs, the bureaucrats and the military officers came from the former warrior class. Social and other legislation was designed to retain as much as possible of the old social structures and attitudes and to maintain essentially authoritarian social relationships. The education system, the armed forces and the administration were mobilised to instil in the population instinctive loyalty to the emperor and to the state.

This social conservatism was particularly marked in the

case of women. A form of official orthodoxy which was spread by the authorities from the 1890s envisaged the role of women as 'good wife, wise mother' (*ryōsai kembo*). According to this orthodoxy, the woman's place was firmly in the home, acting as wife and mother, whilst the duty of the husband was to work. This was reinforced by the increasing exclusion of women from rigorous education and from political and other public activities and, in 1898, the new Civil Code placed women in the family under the authority of men.

Economic and social changes which took place in Japan after the Meiji restoration made it impossible to maintain the old social structures and attitudes as the leaders would have wished. Industrial development and the rapid growth of railways after 1880 marked the beginning of the great migration from rural Japan into the towns and cities. This geographical movement was accompanied by social mobility as former peasants were employed either in the modern factories or in the more traditional urban sectors of the economy. The development of industry involved the creation and growth of an urban industrial workforce. In heavy industry, the workers were almost entirely male but in the textile industry, which by the beginning of the twentieth century was the most important single industry in Japan, the overwhelming majority of the mill workers were women, usually brought into the cities from the countryside. Until the 1930s more than 50 per cent of industrial workers were women. Although there was a very high turnover in women workers, most of them returning to the countryside after a short time in the mills, the changing role of women had its impact upon their position in society. Despite the official obstacles placed in their path, well-to-do women were educated, often to university level. Particularly after the First World War, in the relatively liberal 1920s, many women rebelled against their subordinate position in Japanese society, creating the phenomenon of the 'modern girl', sophisticated and influenced by the cultural tide which swept in from the west. Younger, better-educated males also reacted against restrictive social traditions to create the 'modern boy'. The repression and assertive traditionalism that came to dominate Japanese life in the 1930s arrested many of these social trends but in urban Japan at least they were only partially reversed.

The Origins of Parliamentary Government in Prewar Japan

The leaders of the Meiji state which emerged from the feudal *coup d'état* in 1868 had no clear blueprint for action. Their immediate priorities were to create an effective central administration, which had not existed under the shogun, and a national army. Close study of conditions in Europe and North America convinced the Meiji oligarchs that renovating the economy, especially industrialisation, was an essential base for military power. Traditional attitudes also thrust educational reform into the forefront of the new government's agenda. Reform of Japan's political system at first occupied a relatively low priority for the Meiji oligarchs, but there was a place for it. Power and patronage in the new government was monopolised by former *samurai* from the two largest of the domains that had brought down the shogun. Naturally, this grated with the interests of many who were excluded from power and did not enjoy government patronage. A tide of resentment against the regime built up which manifested itself in two different forms. In the 1870s the leadership received a series of frights caused by rebellion by those whose interests were damaged by the new government's policies, including overtaxed peasants and socially alienated former *samurai*. After the dangerous Satsuma rebellion of 1877 was put down by the new government army there were no serious armed threats to the Meiji regime. The other manifestation of opposition to the new government left much deeper and more permanent marks. In the 1870s a vocal, although not very effective, movement arose, demanding constitutional government under the slogan of 'freedom and people's rights'. This movement helped to focus the government's attention upon political reform. The Meiji oligarchy, who held the levers of power, had no fundamental opposition to the idea of a constitution. The leadership was anxious to widen the bases of support for the new government, and its radical policies, by involving a broader segment of the (male) population in political processes. The more powerful influence on the oligarchs, however, was the hope that introducing a political system modelled upon western patterns would help to have Japan accepted as an equal of the western powers and contribute to the abolition of the unequal treaties. In 1878 the government set up provincial assemblies, intended to draw the support of the well-to-do behind its policies. From 1880, the leadership were engaged in producing a constitution for Japan but it was delayed by disagreements amongst the oligarchs on the precise nature of a national constitution, and the form of the political system that it would create (Akita, 1969).

The constitution finally promulgated in 1889 was largely based on that of Bismarck's Germany and was a politically conservative document. It asserted the ultimate authority of the emperor and was aimed at maintaining the leadership's grip on the reins of government. Large segments of state power resided in the executive, and safeguards were built in to preserve the authority of the state and curb the power of parliament. Despite its conservative intentions, the constitution did set up a parliament of two houses for Japan, one of which, the House of Peers, was an hereditary institution which might be counted upon to limit the power of the lower House of Representatives. The House of Representatives was to be elected on a very narrow franchise achieved by imposing a severe property qualification on the right to vote and excluding women from the franchise. Its only real power lay in control over the budget, but even this was hedged in by a qualification, copied from the German constitution, which allowed the government to levy the previous year's budget if parliament refused to vote a new one.

15

The framers of the constitution intended to keep state power largely concentrated in the hands of the government and the bureaucracy. But the constitution was part of Meiji Japan's long-term strategy to gain acceptance from the western powers and, more practically, to end the unequal treaties, by projecting an image of Japan's politics as being similar to those of contemporary Europe. Thus it was not really a policy option to destroy the constitutional framework if it did not fulfil the government's objectives. Also, the constitution's creators were naturally reluctant seriously to amend, let alone abandon, the constitution since this would be a public admission that their handiwork had been fatally flawed.

The Drift towards Parliamentary Democracy

Japan held its first general election in 1890. The parliament which resulted both surprised and alarmed the Meiji leadership. The policies of the government, and the monopoly of power by men from a small number of old feudal domains, had alienated a wide range of the politically articulate population. The newly elected lower house of parliament was fiercely critical of the government and its policies, and proved truculent when it came to voting budgets. Government expenditure rose rapidly in the 1890s and 1900s because of expansionism and war. The device of hedging the lower house's power over the budget proved ineffective because the previous year's budget was never inadequate to cover the following year's expenditure. In addition, the most vociferous critics of the government began to band together into embryonic political parties. The government tried the ploy of dissolving parliament and using coercion to obtain the election of a more conciliatory assembly, but this tactic did not have the desired result.

Towards the end of the 1890s, the government and some of the young political parties began to turn away from the politics of confrontation and towards the politics of co-operation. In 1898 there was a short-lived cabinet, the majority of whose members came from a political party, the Kenseitō. This cabinet soon fell apart and the Kenseitō itself split, but it was clear that the government would have to build support within parliament. In 1900 the government sponsored the creation of the Seiyūkai, a political party intended to provide parliamentary support for the government. Under its dynamic leader, Hara Kei, the Seiyūkai extended its influence beyond parliament into the provinces and within the bureaucracy. Parliamentary politicians who were not in the Seiyūkai went through a long and complex series of political manoeuvres which culminated, in October 1916, in the creation of a new political party, the Kenseikai, which was nominally more liberal than the Seiyūkai. Thus from 1916 Japan had the bones of a two-party political system. Hara Kei pursued a policy of co-operation and compromise with the old Meiji oligarchs, whose numbers by this time were being thinned out by death and whose survivors were becoming too old to play an active part in politics.

Hara Kei occupied a number of important ministries before becoming prime minister in September 1918, the first party leader to occupy the post. When Hara was assassinated in November 1921, the principle of the prime minister being the leader of the largest party in the elected house of parliament temporarily receded, and cabinets made up of bureaucrats and non-party figures returned. However, all four of these cabinets fell when they lost the confidence of the House of Representatives. In June 1924 the leader of the Kenseikai majority in parliament, Katō Takaaki, was appointed prime minister, an apparent vindication of the principle that the office should go to the leader of the majority party. The fundamentals of parliamentary cabinet government seemed to have been planted in prewar Japan. In the period up to 1932 Japan did take steps in the direction of liberal democracy, but Japan did not become a fully fledged parliamentary democracy (Scalapino, 1962).

Taishō Democracy

The central objective of US policies during the postwar occupation was to 'democratise' Japan. The Americans sought to accomplish this by drawing upon those democratic forces that had appeared in the so-called Taishō democracy of the 1920s. In 1925 the Kenseikai government of Katō Takaaki honoured its commitment to widening the franchise by passing the Universal Suffrage Law which gave the vote to virtually all males over twenty-five. This was the pinnacle of the period of Taishō democracy, named after the emperor who reigned from 1912 to 1926. There were a number of forces at work which led Japan's political system to evolve in the direction of parliamentary democracy. Naturally, it was a direct consequence of the promulgation of the constitution in 1889, although not one sought by that constitution's creators. In the twenty-five years after the constitution was implemented, ultimate state power was held by the *genrō*, a group of 'elder statesmen' initially comprising the leaders of the Meiji restoration, but after 1900 including some of their protégés. The *genrō* exercised considerable influence in strategic policymaking and chose the prime minister. Nature, however, steadily whittled away the elder statesmen. When Yamagata Aritomo died in 1922 the only surviving *genrō* of significance was Saionji Kinmochi, and he was relatively liberal. The passing away of the *genrō* created a political and constitutional vacuum into which the political parties moved.

The enormous changes in Japan since the Meiji restoration had produced momentous social and intellectual changes, many of which were broadly supportive of liberal democracy. The First World War had also created a social and intellectual climate highly conducive to democracy. By the 1920s, important sectors of Japanese society, particularly the urban, westernised, educated middle classes and the young, were so heavily influenced by political and intellectual trends from abroad that they put their support behind the 'Taishō democracy'. The defeat of Germany and

Austria-Hungary during the First World War, widely interpreted as a defeat for militarism, and the failure of the military-led, expansionist foreign policies pursued by Japan during and immediately after that war, temporarily eroded the political influence of the army and navy. Conversely, the fact that the victors in the First World War were parliamentary democracies increased popular support for liberal democratic forms of government amongst the urban and middle-class sections of Japan's population (Duus, 1968).

The high hopes of supporters of the Taishō democracy were ultimately disappointed; within eight years the principle of party government was broken. In a number of ways, the prewar political parties were responsible for their own demise. Neither of the major parties had very much of an ideological or principled basis other than a vague conservatism. Japanese party governments were not noted for their political liberalism; for instance, the Katō government that introduced universal male suffrage also enacted the Peace Preservation Law, a repressive measure intended to suppress left-wing parties but which was also used against liberals. The conduct of the political parties themselves was frequently scandalous and corrupt. Parliament was regularly the scene of extreme rowdyism, and even violence, whilst the evidence of corruption appalled many. The involvement of big business in politics, one of the distinctive characteristics of the postwar political scene, has its origins in prewar Japan. As the political parties emerged, the *zaibatsu* developed close connections with them and helped finance them. Mitsubishi became loosely associated with the Minseitō, the successor of the Kenseikai, whilst Mitsui gravitated towards the Seiyūkai, although all of the *zaibatsu* hedged their political bets and avoided being too closely linked with any political party for fear of the repercussions should the other party gain office (Teidemann, 1971).

The general public, and the all-important military, viewed the close connections between party politicians and the *zaibatsu* as profoundly corrupt. This played upon a fundamental weakness in the political parties caused by their failure to build any popular base of support. They remained largely élite groups with few connections with the mass of society. In fairness to the party politicians, it should be emphasised that the party governments had to grapple with very serious problems. Economically the 1920s was a difficult decade for Japan, culminating in the onset of the great depression. In common with governments in Europe and North America, Japanese party governments were unable to solve these problems, and consequently found their popular support ebbing away. On top of these economic difficulties, Japanese interests in China, widely seen as vital in maintaining Japan in the status of a great power, were under increasing pressure from the rising tide of Chinese nationalism. The party governments were perceived by the military, and others, as inadequate defenders of those vital national interests. Lastly, the Japanese political parties had to compete for political power with two other institutions – the bureaucracy and, above all, the military.

The Bureaucracy in Prewar Japan

The senior civil service was one of the most powerful institutions in prewar Japan, and the bureaucracy was to retain, indeed enhance, its position and influence after the Pacific War. This influential professional bureaucracy was heir to a considerable tradition. During the long Tokugawa peace, the ruling *samurai* had been transformed into a bureaucratic class. After 1868 the new regime not only needed a national army to protect it, but also a national administrative machine to frame and implement its policies. Consequently, one of the first priorities of the new government was to build a bureaucratic machine. Those administrators who emerged were, like the soldiers and sailors, formally the direct servants of the emperor; they were also regarded as one of the legitimate heirs of the *samurai* class and its values. These factors bestowed great prestige and considerably independence on the modern bureaucracy. Its reputation was complemented by the introduction of public examinations for the higher civil service in 1887; after 1893 only those who passed these examinations were eligible for top bureaucratic posts. Senior bureaucrats were recruited from the most able and best educated in the land, giving them a formidable image in a society which put such store on education.

In Meiji Japan there was no sharply drawn distinction between government and administration, so the bureaucracy came to enjoy a considerable political position which was hardly eroded by the rise of the political parties. When the political parties came to dominate cabinets during the period of Taishō democracy, these governments tended to share their influence with senior bureaucrats, upon whom they relied for expertise. The incorruptibility of the higher civil service contrasted uncomfortably with the venality of party politicians, and in the public mind the former enjoyed a renown close to that of the military. A significant number of senior bureaucrats were influenced by the growing tide of ultra-nationalism in the 1930s. Between 1932 and 1945 Japan was to a considerable extent ruled by an informal military–bureaucratic coalition, whilst the role of party politicians in government steadily diminished (Spaulding, 1971).

The End of Party Government

Serious domestic and foreign problems buffeted Japanese party governments in the latter part of the 1920s and into the early 1930s. In 1927 the already fragile economy was rocked further by a serious banking crisis which, although eventually resolved, seriously damaged the party government's reputation for sound administration. In 1930 the world depression hit Japan hard. The impact of the depression was magnified by the decision taken by the government of Hamaguchi Osachi in 1929 to return to the gold standard, further eroding confidence in party rule. The economic

21

downturn in the United States virtually killed Japan's silk exports and this had a devastating effect on rural areas, where more than half the population of Japan still lived and worked. Domestic issues alone caused the popularity of the party governments to plummet. It was foreign problems, however, and consequent difficulties with the military, that put an end party government in prewar Japan.

The Military in Imperial Japan

The enormous importance that the armed forces had in Meiji Japan, and the intimate involvement of some of the Meiji oligarchs with the military, bestowed upon the army and navy an extraordinarily powerful and influential position. Both the army and navy ministers in a cabinet had to be army and navy officers, although between 1913 and 1936 they could be retired officers. The so-called Right of Supreme Command, based on the legal fiction that the military was responsible only to the constitutionally all-powerful emperor, rendered the army and navy virtually independent of political, or any other, control; they were very much powers unto themselves. The rank and file of the armed forces were theoretically forbidden to engage in political activity but in reality this ban was ineffective. It was common for military figures to occupy the premiership and other important offices of state. Even during the high point of democracy in prewar Japan, a retired general, Tanaka Giichi, was prime minister between 1927 and 1929. The armed forces bolstered their institutional and legal power by sinking roots deep into society through a combination of conscription, veterans' associations run by the military and the extension of military training into schools.

During the high tide of Taishō democracy in the 1920s a number of issues caused the military to become progressively disgruntled. The mood of anti-militarism which affected intellectuals and the urban middle classes, fear of

22

a rising left-wing tide amongst the urban working class and the growing power of the Soviet Union in north-east Asia combined to convince many officers that the Japan they had sworn to defend was under threat. The navy was deeply troubled by the politicians pushing through arms limitation, which they interpreted as a dangerous erosion both of national security and of their own position and functions. Many officers were perturbed by Chinese nationalist attacks on Japan's position in China, especially in Manchuria, and felt that inadequate civilian party governments were failing to defend Japan's rights and interests. In addition, many of the most influential officers, particularly in the army, believed that a conflict between Japan and either the Soviet Union or the United States was inevitable. Japan should prepare for this by mobilising Japanese society and economy and by securing control of vital strategic materials on the Asian mainland. Most officers felt genuine concern for the plight of their men's families as the economic difficulties bit deep into rural Japan from which most conscripts came. Those tendencies attracted significant numbers, especially army officers, to so-called 'renovationist' ideologies which advocated revolutionary solutions to Japan's problems, both domestic and foreign (Butow, 1961).

Anxieties and tensions within the army spawned a conspiracy in Japanese units charged with protecting Japan's interests in southern Manchuria. In September 1931 this section of the Japanese army fabricated an incident with the Chinese at Mukden, the Manchurian capital, and used it as a pretext to begin the takeover of Manchuria. The party governments in office were unable either to control the independent action of the army, or to deal with the international repercussions of this Manchurian crisis. At the end of 1931, the machinations of the army in Manchuria forced the resignation of the civilian government of Wakatsuki Reijirō, whose foreign minister, Shidehara Kijūrō, would be prime minister in the crucial year following the surrender in 1945. Another party politician, Inukai Tsuyoshi, succeeded Wakatsuki as prime minister. By early 1932 there was not only conflict in Manchuria, resulting in serious international complications with the western powers, but also severe economic difficulties, plots engineered by extremists and a campaign to whip up popular support behind the army's action in Manchuria. The highly charged atmosphere led to violence: in May 1932 Inukai was assassinated and no other party leader would be prime minister until after the end of the Pacific War.

The last of the *genrō*, Saionji Kinmochi, now chose a retired admiral, Saitō Makoto, as prime minister to head a 'cabinet of national unity'. This government included representatives from the political parties, the bureaucracy and the military. The Saitō cabinet was the first of a series of new 'transcendental' cabinets, so called because they were held to be above party and factional interests. In these cabinets the number of posts occupied by party politicians decreased steadily whilst government power and functions were increasingly turned over to the bureaucracy and the military. The crises of the 1930s gradually eroded party politics, and in November 1940 all the political parties were cajoled into joining the Imperial Rule Assistance Association (*Taisei Yokusankai*) which although never a united, homogeneous organisation none the less put a formal end to normal politics until 1945 (Shillony, 1981).

The Roots of Disaster

Between 1894 and 1910 Japan became a formidable world power. The defeats inflicted on China in 1894–5 and, spectacularly, Russia in 1904–5 made Japan the most powerful nation in east Asia, courted by the other great powers and playing an increasingly important role in the region's international politics. At the same time, Japan became an important colonial power. Taiwan was the fruit of victory over China in 1895. The defeat of Russia in 1905 brought control of Korea, which formally became a Japanese colony

24

in 1910. Japan also gained control of the Kwantung Peninsula and of Russia's political and economic sphere of influence in southern Manchuria. Japan's reward for siding with the victorious allies during the First World War was a League of Nations' mandate over the former German colonies in the Caroline, Mariana and Marshall islands, projecting Japanese power into the central Pacific.

Japan's emergence as a powerful, expansionist state on the western shores of the Pacific raised foreboding on the eastern shores of the Pacific. Until the end of the Russo-Japanese War, American policy and public opinion had been, if anything, sympathetic to the Japanese. The slide into US–Japanese enmity was the product of the rapid rise of a potential future threat to the United States on the other side of the Pacific, combined with burgeoning racial prejudice against the Japanese in the western states and romantic popular attachment to the cause of China, where Japan had joined the other major powers in carving out privileges. This hostility became intense during the First World War, leading pundits in both countries to predict imminent war between Japan and the United States. By 1916 both Japan and the United States had embarked on naval expansion programmes clearly aimed at the other, and collision seemed a likely outcome. A clash was averted by the entry of the United States into the First World War on the side of the Allies in 1917. None the less, American suspicions were kept simmering by Japanese attempts to take advantage of the preoccupation of the European powers and the United States with the war to expand its own position, first in China and then, after the Bolshevik revolution in Russia, in Siberia. Following the end of the First World War some of the venom in Japanese–American relations was drawn, especially by the international conference held in Washington in 1921–2. For the rest of the 1920s US–Japanese relations were perfectly correct, but the wariness between them survived to provide a fertile soil for the flowering of hostility and conflict after 1931 (Morley, 1971).

The Road to the Pacific War

On the night of 18 September 1931 officers of the Kwantung Army, the Japanese army in southern Manchuria, exploded a tiny bomb on the Japanese-owned South Manchurian Railway near Mukden. Without authority from the army high command in Tokyo, and certainly without the knowledge or permission of the government, the Kwantung Army used their own bombing as a pretext to attack the Manchurian army, first in Mukden, and then throughout Manchuria. By 1932 the army, which the government proved incapable of controlling, had put much of Manchuria under its control and created its own puppet-state of Manchukuo. This Manchurian crisis precipitated the end of party government in Japan, beginning the slide to full-scale war with China in 1937 and, ultimately, with the United States and Britain in 1941.

The chief engine for Japanese expansionism in the 1930s and 1940s was the armed forces, particularly the army, but members of the bureaucracy, party politicians, businessmen and, so far as can be judged, the bulk of the population supported Japan's activities on the Asian continent. The reasons for this expansionism were varied and complex, ranging from ethereal idealism to hardheaded pragmatism and selfishness. Many Japanese officers, bureaucrats and politicians were pan-Asianists who genuinely believed that it was their duty to liberate Asia from the oppression of the white colonial powers and lead their Asian neighbours along the same path of development that Japan had trodden after 1868. Such idealism, however, was studded with much more practical considerations. The nature and outcome of the First World War had convinced many Japanese officers that the next war would be long and that victory would depend to a large extent on control of vital raw materials, and on the strength of the combatants' economies.

Many Japanese before 1945 had a sense that Japan's economy was flawed by its lack of control of vital raw materials and of markets for its products. In addition, it was commonly believed that Japan was seriously overpopulated and in need of more territory into which to decant its surplus population. Hence one of the mainsprings of Japan's expansionism in the 1930s and 1940s was a quest for autarky, for guaranteed supplies of vital raw materials. (This sense of economic insecurity has been a recurrent theme in modern Japan. In 1973, fears that Japan's economic structure was seriously undermined by a reliance on foreign suppliers of vital materials caused panic buying by the public, leading to the famous famine of toilet paper.) Idealism and economic and strategic pragmatism came together with the declaration of a pan-Asianist 'New Order in East Asia' in 1938 and its supplementing by the 'Greater East Asia Co-Prosperity Sphere' in November 1940, in which Japan would control the resources of east and south-east Asia (Barnhart, 1987).

Catastrophe

A few minutes before 8 a.m. on Sunday, 7 December 1941 the Japanese naval air force attacked the US Pacific fleet at anchor in Pearl Harbor, close to Honolulu in the Hawaiian islands. Soon afterwards the Japanese attacked the US territory of the Philippines and also assailed the British in Malaya and Burma, and the Dutch in the Netherlands East Indies. Pearl Harbor was the culmination of a decade of gathering Japanese–American confrontation and inaugurated a brief period of almost unprecedented Japanese military triumph which ultimately collapsed into catastrophe for Japan.

Stung by international criticism of its activities in Manchuria Japan left the League of Nations in 1933, heightening a sense of national isolation and insecurity. Also in 1933, Japan forced China to bring the Manchurian 'incident' to an end, although this proved to be truce rather than a peace. In Japan itself, the national mood and internal turbulence in the armed forces culminated in a serious army mutiny in February 1936, serving to strengthen the role of the military, and of nationalists, in the government. Following a minor incident between Japanese and Chinese troops near Peking in July 1937, Japan staggered into a full-scale war with China which sucked men and resources into an attempt to subjugate the Chinese Nationalist government, putting China and its resources fully under Japanese control. The Japanese military occupied vast tracts of north and central China, but in doing so they clashed directly, and sometimes deliberately, with the western powers, especially with Britain and the United States.

Japan's expansionism on the Asian mainland, first in Manchuria and then in China proper, provoked a rising tide of US anxiety and opposition, but there was no resolute response from a deeply isolationist America beset by dire economic problems following the world depression. The growing threat from Nazi Germany after 1933 meant that Britain had to concentrate its strength in Europe and could play no significant part in resisting Japanese expansion; in any case, east of Suez Britain was hopelessly weak militarily. The Americans blustered against Japanese actions, but made no concrete response. The outbreak of war in Europe in 1939, especially the fall of France and the prospect of imminent British defeat in the summer of 1940, was seized on by Japan as an opportunity to begin moving into south-east Asia, prior to asserting control over the oil and other raw materials in the region. In August 1940 Japan forced the prostrate French to allow the Japanese army to occupy the northern part of French Indochina. Politically, the Japanese government moved closer to Nazi Germany, believing that Japan would have to have an understanding with the Germans in the coming carve-up of the British, French and Dutch colonial possessions in south-east Asia. In September 1940 Japan concluded the Tripartite Pact with Germany and Italy, which firmly tied it into the Axis alliance (Iriye, 1987).

In 1939 the United States had begun to impose economic sanctions on the Japanese by abrogating the United States–Japanese Commercial Treaty. In 1940 America began to embargo the export of specialist metals and other strategic materials to Japan. The Tripartite Pact coincided with a decisive shift in American public opinion against Nazi Germany and in favour of a beleaguered Britain. Japan's open alignment with the Axis provoked an even stronger wave of anti-Japanese feeling in the United States. From April 1941 there were desultory negotiations between the Japanese and US governments to try to find a way out of the growing confrontation, but they made no serious progress. The German invasion of the Soviet Union on 22 June 1941 presented Japan with a fateful decision. The Germans urged their Japanese allies to attack the Soviet Union but Japan would make no great economic or strategic gains by war with the Soviets. Instead, the government and the military opted for 'southern' expansion, into south-east Asia. This decision propelled Japan into the final confrontation with the United States. To strengthen their strategic position in south-east Asia the Japanese marched into the southern part of French Indochina in July 1941. The United States, Britain and the Netherlands responded by effectively embargoing oil supplies to Japan. Japan did not have independent access to significant oil reserves and the American-led embargo threatened Japan with the grim choice either of giving in to US demands and surrendering most, if not all, that had been obtained by force since 1931, or using force to seize the raw materials it needed. The second option meant war.

In a series of conferences the decision-making élite pondered the problem. If Japan gave in, it would have been grim confirmation of the long-held fear that Japan was not in reality a truly great power because it was vulnerable to resource blackmail. The emperor used what influence he had in favour of avoiding conflict, but US intransigence made this impossible. On 6 September 1941 the decision was made. If the United States maintained its obdurate attitude, Japan would seize what it wanted even though this inevitably meant war with the United States and Britain (Ike, 1967). In October 1941 Tōjō Hideki, a general of bellicose temperament, became prime minister. There would be no negotiated settlement. The Japanese leadership believed that the Americans lacked the moral fibre necessary to mount an arduous counter-attack and grind down the great defensive line which initial Japanese victories would create. Ultimately, the United States would be forced to acquiesce in Japan's actions. After final hesitations, Japan attacked the United States, Britain and the Netherlands (Butow, 1961).

Japan was spectacularly successful in the first six months of the Pacific War. The British colonies of Malaya and Burma were conquered and India was threatened; the Dutch East Indies, with its rich oil fields, quickly fell to the Japanese. The United States colony of the Philippines was overrun and General Douglas MacArthur, the American commander in the Philippines, was forced to flee to Australia. The battered and weakened Allied forces were unable to resist the Japanese onslaught. The amazing early victories seemed to justify the risk of war, but Japan was no real match for the United States in terms of organisational capabilities and the war potential that industrial power and technological and sophistication bestowed. The Americans did not lack the staying power required to wear down Japan's Pacific bastion, and from the middle of 1942 the weight of American superiority began to be felt. The United States simply out-produced their Pacific enemy, enabling heavier and heavier applications of weaponry and technological innovation to grind the Japanese down. The war in the Pacific was a grim and terrible one. The combatants viewed each other with almost unprecedented depths of racial hatred, and mercy was rarely granted.

The most effective submarine campaign in the history of warfare destroyed a vast proportion of Japan's merchant fleet and virtually cut Japan off from the raw materials that it had gone to war to obtain. On 26 November 1944 the Americans began their strategic bombing campaign against the Japanese mainland which, after a faltering start, built up to a terrible crescendo. On 10 March 1945 over 100,000 people were killed during a raid on Tokyo. In April 1945 the Americans landed on Okinawa, the first part of the Japanese home islands to be invaded. Following a hideously bloody campaign, Okinawa fell to the Americans and the allies prepared for the invasion of the Japanese home islands (Spector, 1984). This potential horror was averted by the dropping of the atom bombs on Hiroshima and Nagasaki on 6 and 8 August, and the Soviet declaration of war on Japan on the same day as the Nagasaki bombing. These events cemented together an alliance of bureaucrats, moderate army and navy commanders, and the emperor, which, on 14 August 1945, was able to push through the decision to accept the Potsdam Declaration that the Allies had issued on 26 July 1945 and surrender without conditions. The emperor's broadcast the following day announced this surrender to a stunned populace (Sigal, 1988).

The Pacific War had a devastating effect on the fabric of Japan's society, economy and politics. Perhaps 8,000,000 Japanese were killed or wounded during the war, whilst 2,500,000 houses had been destroyed or damaged. In Tokyo alone, 709,906 buildings had been destroyed or heavily damaged, and flight from the city had reduced its population from 6,700,000 in 1940 to 2,800,000 in 1945 (Kosaka, 1972). The war and defeat cost Japan some 41.5 per cent of its national wealth: all assets put into military production and activity had been lost, whilst 25 per cent of 'peaceful assets' had been destroyed. Further, Japan would be dispossessed of its colonial empire, along with all the resources that had been invested in it. National wealth at the end of the war was barely greater than it had been in 1935. The Pacific War had cost Japan the value of all of the substantial economic development which had taken place in the decade before surrender. The picture was not entirely black, however: Japan had been spared a land campaign, which would have brought even greater devastation to its industrial and other facilities. US bombing tactics had also partially spared Japan's industrial infrastructure. The high proportion of incendiary, compared to demolition bombs, used had wrought terrible havoc amongst the flimsy housing in

Japan's cities but less than half of the tonnage of bombs dropped on Japan had been aimed at industrial targets. Factories, shipyards, steel mills and the communications infrastructure were less severely damaged than was at first feared (Roberts, 1973). Japan's political structure faced an uncertain future, as did the emperor himself. On 15 August 1945, the outlook for Japan was bleak indeed.

2

GUIDED REVOLUTION: THE OCCUPATION OF JAPAN 1945-52

When he announced the surrender of Japan on 15 August 1945, the emperor warned his subjects that they would have to 'bear the unbearable, tolerate the intolerable'. The greatest unbearable and intolerable fact would be an Allied occupation of Japan. The government had accepted the conditions laid down by the victorious Allies on 26 July 1945 in the Potsdam Declaration. Japan's armed forces were to be disarmed and demobilised, Japan would lose its overseas empire, those held responsible for the war punished, and Japan was to be occupied by the Allied powers, who declared their intention to create 'a new order of peace, security and justice' based on democracy and personal freedoms. The occupation of Japan would end only when all of these objectives had been achieved and 'there had been established in accordance with the freely expressed will of the Japanese people a peacefully inclined and responsible government'. For the first time in its recorded history, Japan would be ruled by outsiders.

The United States and the Occupation

The Americans were surprised both by the timing and nature of the end of the war against Japan. It had been assumed that Japan would be occupied gradually following an Allied invasion of the Japanese home islands and a savage land campaign.

33

Instead, surrender came suddenly, a result of the dropping of the two atomic bombs on Hiroshima and Nagasaki, the Soviet declaration of war on Japan on 8 August 1945, and the appreciation amongst sections of Japan's military and civilian élites that the war was all but lost. On 19 August 1945 a Japanese delegation arrived in Manila to arrange the details of the beginning of the occupation. When the first US contingent arrived at Atsugi naval airbase, close to Tokyo and Yokohama, on 26 August, such was the level of destruction and chaos that the Americans had to use a fire engine to get to Yokohama. Days before the Japanese surrender, President Harry S. Truman had decided that the supreme commander of the ostensibly Allied, but really American, occupation would be General Douglas MacArthur. The supreme commander arrived at Atsugi on 30 August, characteristically with maximum panoply and publicity. MacArthur had not been consulted about the strategies and tactics to be used during the occupation, but for a variety of reasons he was determined to make his mark. In many ways he succeeded and MacArthur would become almost synonymous with the occupation (Schaller, 1989).

The sudden, unexpected end of the war and the need to take over Japan did cause great problems, but the United States was not unprepared for the task of occupying Japan. Since April 1942 a variety of organisations in Washington had been drawing up plans for dealing with Japan when the war ended. By 1945, the basic lines of policy were in place, although the details would be worked out during the occupation. The fundamental objective of the occupation and its policies was ostensibly 'to ensure that Japan will not again become a menace to the United States or to the peace and security of the world'. The basic objectives of the occupation were to disarm and demilitarise Japan, to punish those held responsible for the Pacific War and 'democratisation', developing a liberal democratic political system in Japan. In the process, the occupation was aimed at changing Japanese values and behaviour in order to ensure that Japan would in future be pro-American (Ward, 1987).

After the war, the Allies occupied a number of former Axis states, but the occupation of Japan was different to them in a number of basic and important ways. The occupiers aimed to change an entire nation but, unlike Germany, those who planned and supervised the changes in Japan were racially and culturally very different to the occupied. The occupiers also had a remarkable degree of control over the society they were seeking to transform. In execution the occupation of Japan was radically different in nature to the parallel occupation of Germany. Germany experienced a genuinely 'Allied' occupation, with the country divided into zones. Japan was dealt with as a single entity. The divided occupation of Germany led to the emergence of two separate German states; Japan escaped such a disruption of national unity. Equally significant, it was an Allied occupation in name only; in reality, it was a US occupation, and the policies that the occupiers planned and sought to implement were almost exclusively American. Unlike Germany, the Truman administration chose to run Japan indirectly, using a succession of Japanese governments and Japan's existing bureaucracy to implement their decisions. Indirect administration was forced upon the US occupiers largely by a shortage of linguistically trained personnel. It had the important consequence of providing the Japanese authorities with innumerable opportunities to bend, alter, obstruct, delay and, occasionally, even to ignore the occupiers' intentions. Finally, the occupation of Japan was distinguished by the character and ambitions of its dominant figure, General Douglas MacArthur. MacArthur was, and remains, a controversial figure, still revered by many Japanese who see him as the architect of their postwar freedoms and prosperity, whilst ridiculed by others for his bombast and pretensions. He was a man of unusual self-possession who on the one hand regarded himself as something of an idealistic crusader, but who also saw his period as Supreme Commander for the Allied Powers in Japan as a springboard for his presidential ambitions in the United States. Until 1947 at least, MacArthur, whose military rank conveniently could be translated into Japanese as *shogun*, ruled Japan with few effective restrictions upon his authority, either from his own government or from the weak and divided Allied bodies created to oversee the implementation of occupation policies.

SCAP and the Occupation

The Supreme Commander for the Allied Powers and his administration, both known by the acronym SCAP, was the organisation responsible for formulating details of policy and ensuring that the wishes of the occupation authorities were implemented by the Japanese government. SCAP was never a very large organisation: at its maximum strength in 1948 there were only 3,200 American personnel in SCAP (Schaller, 1989), charged with responsibility for a country which, by the end of the occupation, had a population of nearly 86 million. From the beginning of the occupation, SCAP had a problem of expertise. MacArthur filled some of the top echelons of SCAP with members of the so-called 'Bataan Club', officers who had served with him in the Philippines and elsewhere in the Pacific War. Few of these officers had obvious qualifications or knowledge for the tasks that they would undertake. The United States was faced with the problem of providing personnel not only for the immediate occupation of Japan but also to occupy Korea south of the 38th parallel. In the event, the occupation of Japan was stripped of some of its best trained Japanese-speaking personnel who had to be sent to Korea. This serious lack of trained personnel was compounded by the demobilisation which took place in the months following the end of the war; their replacements were widely regarded as inadequate. One major participant in the occupation's reform of the Japanese legal system, a former German lawyer, when admitting to a war department interviewer that he knew nothing of Japan, was astonished by the reply that 'Oh that is quite all right. If you knew too much about Japan, you might be prejudiced. We do not like old Japan hands!' (Oppler, 1976). Some American servicemen of Japanese extraction did serve in the occupation but many of these Japanese-Americans were as bemused as their Caucasian colleagues by the Japanese. One Japanese observer of the occupation has described the methods used by SCAP in dealing with the Japanese government as 'ranging all the way from suggestion, through cajolery, friendly persuasion, subtle intimidation, polite pressure, scarcely veiled coercion, to peremptory commands backed by demonstrations of military might' (Kawai, 1960: 26). This general unfamiliarity with Japan from which most SCAP officers suffered dictated the decision to use indirect rule and further enabled the Japanese to shape the Allied reforms in subtly different directions to those originally intended.

By retaining a Japanese government, and ruling the country indirectly, the Americans handed to the Japanese a considerable input into measures imposed on them. It gave the essentially conservative elements that dominated both government and bureaucracy in Japan the opportunity to blunt the radical intentions of some of SCAP's reforms. The conservative government argued that the institutions of pre-surrender Japan needed reform not replacement. Before Japan's surrender, this view had some support amongst a small group in Washington which had gathered around the prewar US ambassador to Japan, Joseph Grew, but it was rejected by the more influential decision-makers within the Truman administration. During the early phases of the occupation, working arrangements between SCAP and the Japanese authorities were arranged through the Central Liaison Office, which the Japanese had created and which was staffed by Japanese foreign ministry personnel. Although the Central Liaison Office lost influence as the Americans bedded themselves in and became more accustomed to Japan, it provided the Japanese with an early opportunity to influence SCAP policies. Later, Japanese officials became accustomed to the organisation and working of SCAP bureaucracy, and were able to delay and circumvent SCAP intentions. On issues such as constitutional change, dissolution of the great industrial combines and reform of the civil service, the Japanese were able partially or totally to blunt intended change.

The Japanese and the Occupation

The Americans feared large-scale defiance from the Japanese during the occupation. The Japanese had been fanatical enemies whose resistance had intensified in desperation as the allies approached the home islands. Indeed, during the last months of the war, the Japanese military had prepared to use the bulk of the Japanese population in what promised to be a suicidal campaign against an allied invasion. The surrender made national suicide unlikely, although there were justifiable fears that irreconcilable elements within the armed forces would act to reverse the surrender. The appointment of the emperor's cousin, and army general, Prince Higashikuni, as prime minister two days after the surrender was intended to stifle military disobedience, and mercifully the military high command managed to maintain discipline despite desultory attempts by army diehards to maintain the fight (Fukui, 1988).

One of the more baffling aspects of the occupation is that the feared widespread resistance from a hitherto implacable foe did not materialise. The Japanese were unexpectedly quiescent during the occupation, causing their occupiers little serious trouble. There were a number of reasons why most Japanese quietly accepted the occupation. Without doubt, the bulk of the Japanese population were profoundly weary of war by 1944–5. This war weariness was massively fuelled by the savage strategic bombing during the last six months of the war. Normal life and activity in urban Japan had been virtually snuffed out by catastrophic bombing damage and mass panic. After the formal surrender there was no popular stomach to continue the horror. Understandably, the Japanese had feared a harsh, vengeful occupation, similar in kind to those their own imperial forces had inflicted on conquered areas. In the event, many of the occupation policies were widely popular and the conduct of the US and other Allied occupation forces, whilst far less perfect than portrayed at the time, was orderly. As conditions in Japan deteriorated in the aftermath of surrender, the United States was forced to ship food and other vital commodities to prevent the mass starvation which had loomed in the cities. A natural sense of gratitude moved popular sentiment in favour of the occupiers. Nevertheless, the occupiers took no chances with Japanese popular sentiment. SCAP maintained a firm grip on the media, which they used to build a basis of support for their policies; naturally, no breath of opposition to SCAP and its policies was permitted. Also, the emperor was sent on nationwide tours to drum up support for the occupation and its policies.

Fundamentally, there was no great and sustained tradition of opposition to authority amongst the bulk of the population. Repression in imperial Japan had never plumbed the depths of Nazi Germany or the Soviet Union of Stalin, but it had been a conformist and controlled society in which criticism and opposition were systematically, and sometimes ruthlessly, suppressed. Finally, as an officer in SCAP (later one of the most distinguished academic observers of Japanese society) realised, by no means

> had all Japanese experienced the postwar years in the same way. Some suffered greatly, but others benefited. The beneficiaries were not only the black marketeers or those who had hidden stocks but also many simple farmers who were then in control of the most important asset of all – food. And farm families . . . constituted almost one-half the population. (Passin, 1982).

The Changing Nature of the Occupation

The Allies would occupy Japan for nearly seven years, but during this period the nature and policies of the occupation would change. The first phase, from the beginning of the occupation at the end of August 1945 until the middle of 1947, was dominated by the pursuit of the three basic objectives of demilitarisation, democratisation and retribution. General MacArthur and his administration in Japan, acting through the Japanese government, implemented far-reaching, reformist policies in politics, social organisation and welfare, education and the economy. MacArthur was given virtual freedom of action during this period of radical reform. SCAP quite literally controlled access to, and communications with, Japan and they used this power to exclude outside influences. MacArthur could safely ignore the Allied bodies which supposedly supervised the occupation and Washington showed only sporadic interest in Japan. Subtle changes followed the appointment of General George Marshall as secretary of state in January 1947 and the creation of the US Department of Defense in July 1947, under James Forrestal. Neither Marshall nor Forrestal had the ingrained admiration and respect for MacArthur shown by previous incumbents in the Truman administration and they were willing to question the direction he was taking in Japan. In 1947–8, Washington increasingly took control of the making of policy and began to erode MacArthur's independence in order to reverse much of the radical thrust of SCAP's policies. This shift away from the large-scale and penetrating liberal reformism of SCAP was steadily replaced by measures designed to regenerate the Japanese economy so as to ensure that Japan would be preserved from communism and become a rampart of the US security structure in north-east Asia (Schaller, 1985).

The Beginnings of Radical Reform

As he flew to Tokyo on 30 August 1945 MacArthur dramatically expounded what his attentive audience took as his plans for Japan during the occupation. In reality, MacArthur was not giving his subordinates the benefit of his own insights, his performance being based on a policy directive he had received the day before, the 'United States Initial Post-Surrender Policy', formulated by the State–War–Navy Co-ordinating Committee (SWNCC), which framed basic policy in Washington. These instructions laid down the outline policies which were intended to achieve the basic objectives of the occupation; SCAP, personified by MacArthur, were to be left to work out the details.

Disarming and disbanding Japan's large military machine – the most immediate task of the occupation – was accomplished with the minimum of difficulty. The occupiers took the first of many pragmatic and effective decisions and left the Japanese authorities themselves to disarm and disband the seven million men of its armed forces, with SCAP officials merely supervising the process (Harries and Harries, 1987).

The most high-profile aspect of retribution was the trial of those held to be guilty of war crimes. From May 1946 to November 1948 the International Military Tribunal for the Far East in Tokyo tried twenty-eight so-called class-A war criminals who were held to have conspired to bring about the war whilst they held high office. Of the twenty-eight, two died during the trial and one was judged insane. All the other defendants were found guilty; seven, including Tōjō Hideki, were condemned to death and executed, whilst the remainder received prison sentences, sixteen for life. Elsewhere in east and south-east Asia, the erstwhile allies tried the class-B and class-C miscreants who were accused of atrocities and infringements of the laws of war. Nine hundred and twenty Japanese were sentenced to death by the allies, whilst some 3,000 were imprisoned in these trials. The quality of justice meted out by the International Military Tribunal for the Far East and elsewhere was highly questionable, but the trials and their consequences probably had little real impact on ordinary Japanese (Piccigallo, 1979).

The fate of the emperor, and of the emperor system, was closely tied to the question of punishment. European monarchies had been brought down by defeat in both the First and Second World Wars, and Allied public opinion was broadly hostile to Hirohito and the imperial institution. As the nominal head of state of a defeated nation, and as the man in whose name all acts of government had been committed in imperial Japan, the emperor was a prime candidate for the status of a major war criminal. Most US experts involved in wartime planning for post-surrender Japan were cautious about indicting Hirohito or tearing down the imperial institution for two basic reasons. Firstly, they argued that indicting Hirohito would provoke violent popular resistance to the occupation. Secondly, since occupied Japan was to be governed indirectly, the emperor could be used to legitimate the policies and acts of the occupiers. A further complication was that, for obvious reasons, the British opposed abolition of the monarchy in Japan. MacArthur's belief that the emperor could be useful to the occupation decided the issue and he resisted all attempts to indict Hirohito or sweep away the monarchy. MacArthur was reportedly very impressed by Hirohito's demeanour when they met on 27 September 1945, and he resolved to make use of the emperor. Hirohito was required to 'de-deify' himself on New Year's Day, 1946, and the postwar constitution completely removed the (theoretical) royal absolutism of the 1889 constitution. Retaining the emperor and the monarchy undoubtedly avoided serious trouble from the populace, whilst the emperor certainly made the occupation reforms more acceptable to the Japanese. He also may have had a psychological importance by serving as a symbolic bridge between pre- and postwar Japan (Large, 1992).

The Occupation and Japan's Constitution

In 1945 Japan's government and politics were still based on the 1889 constitution. It was by no means clear that this constitution was inherently authoritarian. Japan had not become a truly autocratic dictatorship in the 1930s, although progress towards full parliamentary democracy had been arrested. Thus the prewar constitutional structure had proven capable legally of supporting both a relatively democratic form of government and a relatively authoritarian one. After the war, it could be legitimately argued that the 1889 constitution was basically liberal and that merely amending it could achieve the required 'democratisation'. Alternatively, it was not unreasonable to contend that it was essentially illiberal and anti-democratic and would have to be replaced if true democracy was to be firmly planted in Japan. During the war, Japan specialists in Washington had discussed the institutional changes that might be necessary to democratise Japan, but at the time of the surrender no firm decision had been taken on the fate of the prewar constitution. Experts had not gone beyond a few general principles. US and SCAP policy on Japan's constitutional future crystallised only after the occupation began.

Shidehara Kijūrō, like all Japanese conservatives, sought to preserve as much as possible of prewar Japan. He argued that the 1889 constitution had proved a perfectly satisfactory basis for a liberal democratic state but in the 1930s it had had the misfortune of being hijacked by the military and ultra-nationalists. Hence radical reform, let alone replacement, was unnecessary. In one of his first meetings with the new prime minister on 11 October 1945, MacArthur immediately disabused Shidehara of this comfortable prospect. MacArthur made it clear that he would require substantial liberalisation of the prewar constitution in order to give women the vote and provide constitutional protection for workers' rights. The cabinet immediately created a special commission, headed by Matsumoto Jōji, a prewar politician, and containing Japan's most eminent constitutional experts, to investigate the problem of the constitution. This commission met twenty-two times between the end of October 1945 and the beginning of February 1946 and submitted its draft of a new constitution to SCAP on 8 February 1946.

Whilst the Matsumoto commission pondered the future of Japan's constitutional system, the issue assumed a considerably higher priority for MacArthur and SCAP. On 27 December 1945 the wartime allies' foreign ministers, meeting in Moscow, created two new bodies which were to oversee the occupation of Japan: the Far Eastern Commission (FEC), located in Washington, and the Allied Council for Japan (ACJ), which would be based in Tokyo. MacArthur was jealous of his independence and always strove to minimise interference by his own government in his policies in Japan; naturally, the prospect of Allied oversight was profoundly distasteful to him. What particularly alarmed the General was that, when it became operative, the Far Eastern Commission would have to approve any constitutional changes in Japan. Thus, if SCAP was to shape Japan's constitutional future, the question would have to be resolved before the FEC came to life (Finn, 1992).

MacArthur received no precise instructions from Washington on remodelling Japan's constitution, but in January 1946 he received serious hints of his government's thinking. This evidence of Washington's interest in Japan's constitutional affairs, along with the danger posed by the Far Eastern Commission, threatened MacArthur's cherished monopoly in guiding Japan's future. The proposals for very limited constitutional change which the Japanese government's Matsumoto commission produced at the beginning of February 1946 were far removed from anything envisaged by Washington, and outside intervention became more likely. Prompted by General Courtney Whitney, one of the 'Bataan Gang' and head of SCAP's Government Section, MacArthur decided on immediate action (McNelly, 1987).

On 3 February SCAP's Government Section was instructed to produce a constitution for Japan; from 4 to 10 February twenty-seven Americans, none of them a constitutional lawyer, laboured to produce the legal framework for the future government and political life of Japan. SCAP produced a draft constitution loosely based on the directives on Japan's future that had been sent from Washington since the end of the war. This draft was presented to a shocked Shidehara by General Courtney Whitney on 13 February. A week later, MacArthur threatened the prime minister with a popular referendum if he did not accept SCAP's constitution. Shidehara feared that, if he rejected the constitution, at best SCAP could force the cabinet to resign and replace it with a left-wing government; at worst, the Far Eastern Commission would impose a republican constitution. When the final draft was presented to it on 5 March 1946, the cabinet had no choice but to accept the SCAP constitution, although the Americans gave way to certain Japanese misgivings about their draft constitution, in particular conceding that parliament would have two houses rather than one as the SCAP draft had originally proposed. To ensure popular acceptance, the draft constitution was dressed up as a Japanese government measure and published on 6 March. The constitution was formally promulgated on 3 November 1946 and came into force on 3 May 1947 (Finn, 1992).

The constitution which SCAP produced in 1946 was a conventional expression of liberal democracy, but it had some distinctive features. The preamble and the first chapter set the tone. Sovereignty was firmly rooted in the people and popular sovereignty was entrenched by converting the emperor from the fount of sovereignty, as in the 1889 constitution, to a figurehead constitutional monarch without significant power. The forms of government which the SCAP constitution created bore a marked resemblance to what had emerged in the 1920s. The cabinet system was retained, but it was made inescapably responsible to an elected two-chamber legislature. The House of Representatives would have preponderant legislative power, and the House of Councillors was the more junior of the two houses with largely revising powers; mechanisms were built in to avoid legislative breakdown should the two houses become stalemated.

In order to prevent a repeat of what had happened in the 1930s, the new constitution laid down that the prime minister had to be a member of parliament, that he and his ministers would be civilians, and that the majority of ministers had to be members of parliament. Drawing on the United States constitution, SCAP's document provided a system of judicial review of the government's activities designed to ensure that it acted within the constitution. A series of articles enumerated a large number of human rights for the Japanese, including equality between the sexes, female suffrage, free speech, and political and religious rights, reinforced by a constitutional separation of state and religion. Influenced by US practice, the American writers of the constitution tried to erode some of the authority of the government by devolving some functions to local authorities. This flew in the face of modern Japan's constitutional experience and would be quietly buried in the 1950s.

The most distinctive, and controversial, provision in the postwar constitution was article IX by which Japan renounced war as an instrument of national policy and would be permanently disarmed. The origins and parenthood of article IX have never been satisfactorily explained. One version is that Japan's constitutional renunciation of war, and consequent total disarmament, originated with Shidehara, who was anxious to do everything to preserve the emperor system. He may have felt that he could remove any residual US fears that the emperor might again become the focus for militaristic nationalism by removing the military. The no-war article has also been attributed to idealistic members of SCAP's Government Section, taking advantage of the opportunity to insert the utopian renunciation of war. There is a considerable weight of evidence that MacArthur, virtually alone amongst US policymakers, favoured the total disarmament of Japan; certainly until the outbreak of the Korean War in June 1950 he invariably opposed proposals to rearm Japan. Whoever was the midwife of article IX it was not drafted as a watertight ban on a rearmed Japan, but was sufficiently vague to allow the revival of Japan's armed forces to begin less than five years after it was drafted (Harries and Harries, 1987).

The 1947 constitution changed the constitutional framework of Japan in a number of decisive ways. Japan became a constitutional monarchy, with sovereignty firmly located in the people. The constitutional provisions laying down the nature of parliament and the cabinet's relationship to it firmly established the principle of cabinet responsibility to parliament and ensured the dominance of political parties in the political and decision-making processes. The civil rights of the ordinary citizen were given constitutional force, although some critical observers cast doubt on the real value of this. The system of judicial review, copied from US experience, did not have the same influence as the US Supreme Court; judicial review has not been effective in Japan. In addition, SCAP's attempts to decentralise power did not survive the 1950s. Despite their lack of experience and expertise, the American drafters of postwar Japan's constitution avoided the obvious pitfall of simply transplanting the US constitution to Japan, where previous experience would have rendered it wholly unsuitable. Even a wary observer of postwar Japan's political life has written that the constitution

> was, without a doubt, a very fine and admirable document drawn up by intelligent and caring people who wanted to put the Japanese back on the right path. It contained some of the cleverest mechanisms and loftiest principles.   (Woronoff, 1986: 28)

The Occupation and the Bureaucracy

The American occupiers were able to alter the constitutional system of Japan significantly but they failed to make any appreciable impact upon the civil service. The bureaucracy had been one of most powerful institutions in prewar Japan and had been closely involved in Japan's national policies after 1931. Even in 1946 one SCAP official was appalled to discover that bureaucrats had greater power

47

than elected politicians. As such, it was a prime candidate for both purging and serious reform. Yet no serious attempt was made to purge the bureaucracy. Only 830 (1.9 per cent of those investigated) were actually purged and this represented a rate of one bureaucrat purged for every hundred members of the military. In November 1946 a US mission, led by Blaine Hoover, arrived in Japan and drafted the National Public Servants Law without consulting the Japanese. This law, which would have seriously eroded the power of the civil service, was promulgated in October 1947 but the Japanese bureaucracy was able to subvert its intentions. Hoover supervised a second attempt at legislation in December 1948, but it too was ineffective. The bureaucracy emerged from war and the occupation stronger than it had been before 1945. Its most serious rival for power, the military, had disappeared following defeat, whilst SCAP had inflicted little visible change upon the civil service. Once the decision had been taken for the occupation to exercise power indirectly, through Japanese authorities, the established civil service became indispensable to SCAP. Thus the bureaucracy, which traced its roots to the *samurai* of Tokugawa Japan and had been one of the bastions of conservatism in prewar Japan, survived virtually intact in the postwar era (Baerwald, 1959).

The Occupation and Education

During the Tokugawa era, education and literacy in Japan had grown to levels unusual in a pre-industrial society. One of the first priorities of the Meiji government was to extend this and create a universally educated population. Beginning in 1872, compulsory education was spread steadily to all regions of Japan and all sectors of society. By the early twentieth century Japan had a well-developed system of compulsory state education. The prewar education system was highly élitist and only a small proportion of the population progressed beyond primary school. As with all other state institutions in prewar Japan, the education system was highly centralised and controlled. It had a vital political function. The syllabuses in schools, and even universities, were developed to support the prevailing ideologies of prewar Japan.

Realising the potential of the education system for disseminating their ideas and policies, the American occupiers intended to usurp the political function of education and use it in support of democratisation. SCAP hoped to break central control of education, giving local authorities a decisive role in education. They aimed to introduce a school system modelled on the US schooling pattern with a single point of entry and multiple exits into both employment and higher education. A significant increase in the number of universities and syllabus reform would also greatly increase access to higher education. In March 1946 a US education mission arrived in Japan to draft plans for the reform and extension of education. The reform package which this mission produced was based on the US model. It imposed the so-called 6–3–3–4 pattern, providing six years of elementary education, three years of middle school, three years for high school and four years for a full university course; the first nine years of education would be compulsory. The American plans also stipulated a vast increase in the number of universities and generally gave greater access to higher education. Administratively, the occupiers sought to decentralise control of the schools system. Japanese education officials had no fundamental objections to the SCAP proposals on education, although they were unhappy about devolution of control over the schools and they tried to delay their implementation on financial grounds. SCAP was determined to put the new education structure in place as soon as possible so that it might begin to fulfil its political function. On this occasion, they tolerated no Japanese obstruction and imposed the changes in April 1947. The education reforms were less spectacular than the rewriting of the constitution. After Japan regained its independence the decentralisation of the schools system was reversed, but otherwise, like the constitution, the American-imposed education system remains largely unaltered. The impact of the education reforms on postwar Japan has been enormous. The élitism of the prewar system was rapidly eroded: in 1940 only 7 per cent of the population went to high school; by 1955, under the reformed system, the figure had exceeded 50 per cent, rising to over 95 per cent by 1986. One of the principal sources of Japan's postwar economic growth has been the quality of its workforce. Unquestionably the education system, as reformed by the US occupiers, has been one of the prime factors in achieving this by extending high levels of education into the mass of the population, an achievement that would have been beyond the prewar system. The role of the state education system bequeathed by the occupation has been so valuable that, apart from the reassertion of central control in the 1950s, it has been left virtually intact by postwar Japanese governments (Passin, 1965).

Land Reform

Radical reform of patterns of land ownership was one of the most far-reaching achievements of the occupation. The Americans believed that land reform was vital because the widespread distress experienced by many tenant farmers in the 1920s and 1930s, and the serious landlord–tenant disputes that ensued, had contributed significantly to the growth of extremism, especially amongst army officers who felt a paternalistic concern for their men, who were drawn largely from the peasantry. Land reform had been an issue in Japan since the 1920s and a variety of remedies for the grosser aspects of the maldistribution of land had been proposed. During the war, the peasants' predicament had been partially alleviated by government legislation which aimed to maximise food production by weakening the power of the landlords. The Initial Post-Surrender Directive, sent to MacArthur at the end of August 1945, had spoken of democratising agriculture, but there was little flesh on the bones of this proposal. Initially SCAP showed little detailed concern for land reform, and the early moves came from the Japanese.

In August and September 1945 there were signs that the government was considering land reform, and the Japanese ministry of agriculture prepared draft legislation which it presented to the cabinet in November. The conservative Shidehara cabinet wanted to retain the traditional relationships within rural society as an authoritarian bulwark against left-wing ideologies. It was lukewarm about land reform, watering down its own officials' proposals to reduce their impact upon the landlords. Then, on 9 December 1945, SCAP intervened with a memorandum to the Japanese government requiring radical reform of land tenure arrangements. The Diet, which had been elected in 1942 and was profoundly conservative, was reluctant to pass even the moderate cabinet land reform proposals, but the SCAP intervention frightened them into putting it in to law.

MacArthur's interest in land reform dated from October 1945, after he received a memorandum from Washington on the subject. It is not entirely clear why MacArthur became so enthusiastic an advocate of the radical restructuring of land holding; speculation has it that it was some form of tribute to his father who had been deeply involved with land reform during his period as governor-general of the Philippines. By April 1946 SCAP was signalling that the Japanese government's land reform measure was too moderate, and in June 1946 the cabinet was presented with much more radical proposals. The Shidehara government could only retreat as gracefully as possible and the SCAP-imposed land reform legislation became law on 21 October 1946 (Dore, 1959).

The occupation's land reform was certainly radical. An upper ceiling on the amount of land that could be owned by an individual was fixed at 1 *chō* (2.45 acres) in most of Japan; in Hokkaido the maximum land holding was 4 *chō*. Landowners with more than such small holdings were forced to sell the surplus to the government, which then re-

51

distributed the land. Since the value of the money which landlords received for this land was rapidly destroyed by rampant inflation, the landowners were in reality expropriated. The political significance of this land reform was profound. The reforms gave land to 92.1 per cent of all farmers, and only 7.9 per cent were left landless. Ironically, given the opposition of the conservative Shidehara to radical land reform, the SCAP scheme created a class of small-scale peasant landowners who became the electoral bastion of the conservative parties in postwar Japan.

The political significance of the postwar land reform was immense; without it, it is unlikely that the conservatives could have maintained their dominance of Japanese politics beyond the mid-1950s. Economically, the occupation's land reform did not have an immediate impact. Although there had been massive redistribution of the ownership of land, the unit of production in Japanese agriculture remained – and remains – the very small family farm (Hayami, 1988). It did, however, contribute to a subsequent significant increase in agricultural production, since 'farmers' will to work rose, and the basis for a conspicuous rise in agricultural productivity was created' (Kosai, 1986: 22). This rise in agricultural production was of vital importance to the recovering Japanese economy in the 1950s and into the 1960s (Dore, 1959).

Zaibatsu Dissolution and Economic Deconcentration

The powerful industrial conglomerates, the *zaibatsu*, which had emerged during the process of industrialisation to dominate the modern sectors of prewar Japan's economy, were held to have constituted the economic prop of militarism and ultra-nationalism. Consequently, the American occupiers of Japan intended to act quickly and decisively to break up these conglomerates. By 1945 the ten major *zaibatsu* accounted for 35.2 per cent of the total value of the Japanese economy; the four largest and most famous of them (Mitsui, Mitsubishi, Sumitomo and Yasuda) alone controlled 24.5 per cent of Japan's economic activity. Both the Initial Post-Surrender Policy document sent to MacArthur on 29 August 1945 and the Basic Directive for Post-Surrender Military Government in Japan, which the US Joint Chiefs of Staff dispatched to SCAP on 3 November 1945, required the breakup of the *zaibatsu* in a process euphemistically called economic deconcentration. The assault on the *zaibatsu* began on 6 November 1945 when SCAP demanded the dissolution of the main holding companies (*honsha*) of the four major conglomerates. There were a number of motives behind the American policy of economic deconcentration. The *zaibatsu* were accused of being an important supporter of nationalist expansionism and militarism in the 1930s and 1940s; they had unquestionably been directly involved in the exploitation of those areas conquered by Japan. Further, American economic planners felt that the level of economic concentration which the *zaibatsu* represented had depressed wages, obstructed the emergence of the middle classes and this had been a contributory factor in the growth of extremism before the Pacific War. The *zaibatsu* had been closely involved in Japan's strategic industries, and therefore dismantling them was part of the process of demilitarisation. Finally, anti-trust sentiment, that is opposition to monopolies and oligopolies, was a strong tradition in the United States, especially amongst New Deal liberals who had great influence in framing and implementing the early occupation policies. It might also be mentioned that some Japanese observers suspect that the *zaibatsu* companies which SCAP assailed were targeted because they had posed serious competition to US companies before the Pacific War (Hadley, 1970).

The slow beginnings of MacArthur's occupation had lulled the *zaibatsu* into a false sense of security. The management felt that they would be left relatively undisturbed to profit from the enormous task of reconstruction. The conglomerates' leaders felt they had powerful allies since the formation of the Shidehara cabinet on 9 October 1945 produced a government many of whose most senior members, including Shidehara himself, had close family and professional connections with the *zaibatsu* (Roberts, 1973). Therefore, when it came, SCAP's action took the *zaibatsu* heads by surprise. During October 1945 Raymond Kramer, the head of SCAP's economic section, met representatives of the *zaibatsu*, and proposals emerged which would change patterns of ownership and control by dispossessing the old *zaibatsu* families of the bulk of their holdings and control, but would leave the conglomerates themselves largely unaltered. MacArthur was ready to go along with this plan, but simply changing the ownership and top management of the *zaibatsu* was rather less than Washington had in mind for the future of the great combines.

In December 1945 a further attack was launched on eighteen companies which were deemed to be holding companies for the *zaibatsu*. In April 1946 the Holding Company Dissolution Commission was created which, by June 1947, had dealt with the affairs of eighty-three companies, twenty-eight of which had been liquidated. In addition, SCAP designated over 1,000 plants which were to be used for reparations to Japan's victims, the bulk of which were *zaibatsu* owned. By the end of 1946, however, SCAP enthusiasm for breaking up the *zaibatsu* was waning. The Truman administration in Washington had become deeply alarmed by the impact of economic deconcentration on the prospects for Japan's ultimate economic recovery. As the Cold War set in, many US decision makers feared that continued economic distress in Japan could result in the poverty-stricken population turning to communism. Thus, when the Law for the Elimination of Excessive Concentration of Economic Power was promulgated in April 1947 it was only half-heartedly implemented. 325 firms were designated to be 'deconcentrated' but only eighteen received the treatment. These measures had a fundamental impact on steel, shipbuilding, paper, brewing, and several other industries, but a significant proportion of the geography of industrial power in Japan remained intact. On the other hand, control and management did alter fundamentally. In addition, the economic strategies of the companies which had made up the *zaibatsu* changed. Decisions were no longer made in the interests of the whole *zaibatsu* conglomerate but in the interests of the individual enterprise. Competition amongst former *zaibatsu* members, and the forms of strategic planning that they followed, was a powerful element within the dynamic of economic growth in Japan after 1950. Although economic concentration became more pronounced after the end of the occupation, the old-style *zaibatsu* disappeared and a new and more formidable type of conglomerate, the *keiretsu*, emerged (Kosai, 1986).

The Occupation and the Labour Movement

Some of the liberal policy-makers who were an important influence on early SCAP policy believed that a free, dynamic labour movement would be an important prop for a democratic society in Japan. Labour unions had emerged in Japan at the very end of the nineteenth century but a combination of official repression and internal divisions severely restricted their capacity to penetrate and organise the burgeoning industrial workforce. In particular, the internal divisions which centred on the tension between the far-left leaders, who urged confrontation, and the approach of the centre-left unions, who argued for more conciliatory policies, prevented the unions from capitalising on the relatively liberal decade of the 1920s. In 1931, when union membership was at its zenith in prewar Japan, less than 8 per cent of industrial workers belonged to trade unions. Between 1938 and 1940 the trade union organisations were merged into a state-controlled national labour front and independent workers' organisations effectively disappeared (Garon, 1987).

The trade union enthusiasts within SCAP moved quickly. In December 1945 they pushed through the Labour Union Law which for the first time guaranteed full trade union rights to all Japanese workers. With the initial encouragement of SCAP, and because of the economic hardships of the immediate postwar period and early union successes in negotiating improved wages and conditions, the labour unions grew very rapidly; by 1947 46 per cent of the industrial workforce had become union members (Shimada, 1992). This achievement was marred by a repeat of prewar divisions within the union movement, and the communist and non-communist organisations parted company. In the 1940s the major share of unionised labour belonged to the communist-dominated *Sanbetsu Kaigi*. The newly unionised workforce proved militant and radical. 'Production control' (*seisan kanri*), by which the workers seized control of factories and production from the management, had begun in October 1945 when workers took over the *Yomiuri* newspaper, and it rapidly became a common form of industrial action; in 1946 there would be 255 instances of production control. In October 1946 over one hundred strikes wrung wide-ranging concessions on pay and conditions in many industries (Gordon, 1993). The exploding industrial unrest, and accompanying large demonstrations, was so widespread that some observers concluded that Japan was in such a state of revolutionary fervour that a Japanese people's democratic republic could not be ruled out (Moore, 1983).

The decisive moment came in early 1947. A dispute over wages and bonuses on the Japan National Railways escalated into a threatened communist-led general strike scheduled to begin on 1 February 1947. MacArthur and SCAP were probably less alarmed, and less influenced, by the dangers posed by the radical left than is sometimes thought (Finn, 1992). None the less, the turbulence of the previous year, growing American restiveness with communism and the pleas of the conservative Yoshida cabinet, led MacArthur to ban the general strike. The strike organisers chose not to confront SCAP and the mass political radicalism of the labour movement receded. Immediately, of course, the radical labour movement had been defeated by the intervention of SCAP. Basically it had been wrecked by the innate conservatism of most Japanese workers. A 1946 survey found that the overwhelming majority of employees supported the fundamentally conservative emperor system, and there is evidence that the loyalty of *zaibatsu* employees remained primarily to the corporation and its owners (Fukui, 1988). This was unpromising soil for politically militant, even revolutionary, trade unionism.

The Genesis of Postwar Politics

Since 'democratisation' was one of the fundamental aims of the occupation, SCAP regarded the restoration of normal political life in Japan as vital to their plans. In many ways the centrepiece of the occupation was the constitution, which would put regulated government and politics on a new footing. Also, as the Americans exercised their authority indirectly through the Japanese government the complexion of that government and the political environment in which it operated were central to the occupation. The emergence of new political parties and interest groups and the successful functioning of the new constitutional and other political machinery, were viewed as important symbols of success for the occupation. US fears of the growth of communism, and even of revolution, in Japan gave the occupiers an added urgency in rebuilding party and electoral politics.

Two days after the surrender, a new cabinet was formed. The prime minister was Prince Higashikuni Naruhiko, who as a member of the imperial family and a general was intended to dampen down the possibility of hardline resistance to Japan's surrender. The Higashikuni cabinet was intended only as an interim transitional government. Higashikuni and most of his cabinet were conservative and resigned when, on 4 October, SCAP issued a directive ordering the release of political prisoners and the scrapping of the 'dangerous thoughts' legislation.

The new cabinet formed on 9 October 1945 was presided

over by Shidehara Kijūrō, a veteran diplomat who had been foreign minister when the Manchurian incident began in September 1931. The most pressing priority of Japanese cabinets during the occupation was, of course, negotiating with the Americans. Since this represented a form of foreign policy, former diplomats tended to emerge as prom inent figures in government. Shidehara, who was not in any real sense a party politician, was the first of these diplomat prime ministers. He was followed in May 1946 by another former diplomat, Yoshida Shigeru, who would be prime minister for nearly five of the seven years which the occupation lasted. Shidehara had to handle the myriad demands of the early occupation, including the issue of the constitution. He was a committed conservative, anxious to preserve as much of prewar Japan as possible. His particular obsession was to preserve the institution, and the person, of the emperor, and to this end he would accept almost any proposal that the Americans put to him. Shidehara had a difficult task in his eight months of office. He was a fluent English speaker, careful to establish a good working relationship with MacArthur and other senior SCAP figures. It is difficult to assess the impact that Shidehara had on the early course of the occupation, but it is unlikely that any other prime minister would have been more successful in deflecting the radicalism of SCAP.

In April 1946 Japan held its first general election since 1942. The election had been timed by SCAP so that it would serve as a referendum on its draft constitution. The election was unusual in a number of ways. It had been preceded by a combination of substantial change and utter confusion in Japanese politics. Political parties had begun to emerge following the surrender. The prewar political parties had been compulsorily merged into the Imperial Rule Assistance Association in November 1940, and both the conservative and left-wing parties which materialised after the surrender were their descendants. In November 1945 the Japan Socialist Party (JSP) and two conservative parties, the Japan Liberal Party and the Japan Progressive Party, had been formed; in December another conservative, Japan Co-operative Party, appeared (Thayer, 1969). Many of the new politicians were men who had been active before 1940. The new parties did not reflect a settled political scene. In fact, there was a shifting kaleidoscope of parties and elements swirling around the election, creating a political confusion that was reflected in the 267 political parties which contested Japan's first postwar general election, many of them representing tiny sectional interests. Socially, the 1946 election was significant as the first in which Japanese women voted. Only 19 per cent of those elected to the House of Representatives had been elected to parliament before, so the election marked a vast transfusion of new blood into Japan's politics (Hrebenar *et al.*, 1986).

What emerged was a 'fragmented multiparty pattern' which required negotiations to create a coalition. The complexity was compounded by the SCAP purges of new party members who were held to have been involved in the events of the 1930s and 1940s. These purges, which excluded designated politicians from political activity, were designed to punish those who were believed to have been involved in the extremism of the 1930s and 1940s. They hit the conservative parties especially hard but the JSP was not spared. Hatoyama Ichirō, leader of the Liberal Party, which had won most seats in the election, was on the verge of negotiating a coalition with himself as prime minister when he was purged. The Liberals found a new leader in Yoshida Shigeru but the resulting coalition that he negotiated with other conservative parties was unstable. The first Yoshida cabinet was a lacklustre affair, so lacking in achievement that Yoshida did not mention it in his memoirs, and it barely survived a year. The SCAP reforms were in full spate, and the conservative Yoshida found much of it uncongenial. Divisions within the inherently unstable coalition were exacerbated by problems with the economy, high inflation and growing trade union militancy. None the less, Yoshida's emerging political prominence was of great long-term consequence since it initiated the close relationship between the bureaucracy and the conservative parties which was a distinctive feature of postwar Japanese politics (Dower, 1979).

In April 1947 Yoshida tried to stabilise his government through a general election. In the event, the JSP did remarkably well, polling over 26 per cent of the popular vote and winning the largest number of seats in the House of Representatives. This enabled Katayama Tetsu, the JSP leader, to negotiate a coalition with two of the more moderate conservative parties. This cabinet, the first in Japanese history to be led by a socialist, survived less than ten months. Both the JSP and its conservative partners were riven by factionalism, and the coalition partners had profound policy differences, especially over nationalisation. The government was so split that it was progressively unable to deal with day-to-day problems, hence in February 1948 Katayama gave up and resigned. Japan would wait another forty-six years before it had another socialist prime minister. The leader of the conservative Democratic Party, Ashida Hitoshi, put together another coalition of virtually the same political complexion as the Katayama government and it suffered the same fate, finally falling in October 1948, ostensibly because of the arrest of a prominent member of the JSP for electoral irregularities. In reality it fell because the socialist–moderate conservative coalitions were inherently unstable and the constituent member parties were riven by incessant infighting.

The Americans had regarded Yoshida's first cabinet as both incompetent and reactionary, a government which was naturally opposed to the thrust of SCAP reforms. Following the fall of the Ashida government, the Government Section of SCAP tried to block the emergence of a second Yoshida cabinet and scrabbled round to find an alternative. It failed to do so and Yoshida regained the premiership. Yoshida was prime minister for the next six crucial years of postwar Japan's development and he is justifiably regarded as a major figure in that process. He was remarkably independent of the Americans, who remained wary and suspicious of him, and as 'America's man-in-Japan . . . [who] never nestled complacently in its pocket' (Dower, 1979: 274–5). The beginning of Yoshida's second term of office coincided with increasingly clear indications that the direction of occupation policy was changing

The Reverse Course

The first indications of differences of opinion between US officials charged with planning policies towards postwar Japan had appeared during the war when outline plans were being prepared for the occupation. The so-called 'China Crowd', officials mostly associated with and sympathetic towards China, regarded Japan as potentially a permanent threat to the United States. They urged that the United States should impose a thorough-going programme of fundamental change in an occupied Japan. Ranged against them were the 'Japan Crowd', led by Joseph Grew who had been US ambassador in Tokyo at the time of Pearl Harbor. Grew and his associates argued that Japan would be America's natural postwar ally in the western Pacific, and that Japan's political, economic and social institutions would only require fine tuning to make it an acceptable friend. During and immediately after the war, the 'China Crowd' was dominant in Washington and their views were reflected in SCAP policies. However, a number of factors served to produce a 'reverse course' which increasingly swung US policy into directions essentially similar to the views of the 'Japan Crowd' (Harries and Harries, 1987).

There were a number of interlocking reasons for this 'reverse course' in US policy. First, and most important, the onset of the Cold War, with an accelerating deterioration in US–Soviet relations, led many decision-makers in Washington to view Japan as a vital link in the American world-wide security network which sought to contain the perceived menace of international communism. This analysis demanded a halt to any policy which weakened the fabric of

Japan's fragile economy and society in order to ensure that social alienation and material distress did not cause the Japanese to lapse into communism. Changes in both personnel and decision-making structures in the United States which took place in 1947 were vital in producing these changes since neither General Marshall nor James Forrestal had a high opinion of MacArthur and his works in Japan. The emergence of George Kennan as a key influence on policy-making in Washington thrust to the centre of policy formulation a man who believed that in future Japan would be vital to US policy in east Asia, and that US policy should be designed to recognise and prepare for it. The second reason for the policy shift was to try to ease the burden of the mounting cost to the United States of shoring up Japan. The Japanese economy was in dire straits in the three years following the end of the Pacific War. Between September 1945 and June 1948 the United States was forced to send $1 billion in non-military aid simply to prevent mass starvation in Japan and keep the economy ticking over. Some observers sympathetic to the policies of the United States during the occupation have interpreted the reverse course as an attempt to preserve the basic reforms by improving Japan's economic circumstances and thereby building up popular support for the new structures. Scholars who take a more cynical, or hostile, view of postwar US motives see the reverse course as part of the effort to build a dominant US position in the international economy in which Japan would be tied into a 'US-dominated capitalist system' (Schaller, 1985).

Even before pressure from Washington for a 'reverse course' became irresistible, there were signs in Japan that the liberalism which had marked the early phase of SCAP policy was waning. The purges were rapidly brought to an end. Reparations, which had been an important dimension both of retribution and demilitarisation, were quickly wound down to nothing. The enthusiasm for demolishing the *zaibatsu* quickly evaporated. But it was, of course, the labour movement, which the occupiers had initially encouraged, which had been on the receiving end of the first indication that SCAP policy was being reorientated when MacArthur banned the general strike threatened for 1 February 1947.

SCAP took advantage of their victory at the beginning of 1947 to erode some of the advances that the unions had made in the first eighteen months of the occupation. In doing so, SCAP laid the foundations of the dominant structure of industrial relations in postwar Japan. New labour legislation was passed in 1947 and 1948 to prevent strikes by government employees. The offensive against the unions gained pace following Yoshida's return to power in October 1948. Yoshida was hostile to organised labour and he co-operated with SCAP, now thoroughly imbued with a Cold War mentality, in driving communists and left-wing trade unionists out of the public services in the so-called 'Red Purge' of 1950, and he tried to encourage the growth of moderate unionism.

Most of the trade unions were not organised nationally and did not represent particular occupations and crafts. Instead, they were based upon the companies for which union members worked. These 'enterprise unions' had both blue- and white-collar employees in the same labour union. This enterprise union structure had developed partly because workers had become accustomed to enterprise-based organisation because of the wartime labour front. Also, immediately after the surrender there had been neither time nor opportunity to organise on a craft basis nationwide. Above all, enterprise unionism was the product of the fact that the company was the institution with which the employee most closely identified (Shimada, 1992). This enterprise union would evolve into one of the most distinctive features of postwar Japan's structure of industrial relations.

The Economy During the Occupation

It was hardly surprising that soon after Japan surrendered industrial production ground to a virtual halt. Bomb damage was only a minor cause of this. For instance, in August

1945 there were still eight blast furnaces in operation; by September 1946 there were only three. Between August and November 1945 coal production plummeted from 1,670,000 tons to 550,000 tons. The collapse of industrial production was the result of organisational chaos, lack of raw materials and rampant inflation, some of it induced by governments in 1945. To add to the misery, the rice harvest was the worst since 1903, and by 1946 official rations were only one-fifth of required food intake (Kosai, 1986). Although mass starvation was avoided by SCAP action, a British naval officer 'actually saw someone fall down and die of starvation at my feet in the street'.

Despite enormous casualties of war, unemployment quickly became a serious problem. Some 13 million were either demobilised or repatriated from the old colonial empire, and 6 million were looking for work. Little or no employment was to be found in the cities or the industrial sector, so large numbers took the traditional route in times of urban economic downturn and returned to their families' farms: by 1947 well over 50 per cent of the population were living in or near villages. The loss of the colonial empire meant that Japan was deprived of 46 per cent of its prewar territory. The interlocking relationship between the economies of Japan itself and its colonial territories, which had become increasingly close in the 1930s and early 1940s, was shattered. This further dislocated significant sectors of the Japanese economy (Hirschmeier and Yui, 1981).

SCAP's initial instructions were to take no undue measures to revive the Japanese economy. Indeed, some of the measures intended to achieve the basic objectives of the occupation could only compound the dislocation which the war had inflicted on the industrial and modern service sectors of the economy. Most immediately, the threat of reparations posed a grave danger to Japan's industrial infrastructure. If significant quantities of Japanese industrial plant were shipped as compensation to the victims of Japanese expansionism, the prospects of a recovery would recede into the far distance. In November 1945 a mission under Edwin Pauley arrived in Japan to assess the scale and nature of the reparations to be extracted from Japan. The Pauley mission, which reported to its Washington masters at the end of 1945, took a regional view of its task. Pauley asserted that before 1945 Japan had distorted the economic development of its neighbours. His report recommended that this should be rectified by large-scale transfers of Japanese industrial plant to other parts of east and south-east Asia. Pauley's parting shot was that 'in the overall comparison of needs Japan should have last priority'. Fortunately for Japan's postwar economic prospects, Pauley's draconian reparations plan appeared just as the decision-makers began to alter course. It met resistance in both Washington and Tokyo. The Joint Chiefs of Staff feared that the large-scale transfer of industrial plant would damage the Japanese economy too greatly. MacArthur had obstructed reparations because he feared the consequences of depressing Japanese standards of living and he saw the Pauley report as a thinly veiled criticism of him. In April 1947 Washington forced SCAP to send 16,000 machine tools as reparations to Japan's Asian victims, but MacArthur and his Washington allies were able to ensure that this represented the sum total of reparations made during the occupation (Schaller, 1985).

The policy of breaking up the *zaibatsu* conglomerates posed another threat to the hopes for Japanese industrial recovery. These conglomerates had been central to the working of the prewar economy, and US decision-makers, who were anxious to revive Japan's industrial economy to counter the dangers of communism and to relieve the United States of some of the burden of propping up Japan, pushed for an end to economic deconcentration. Closely tied to the *zaibatsu* question was the issue of the purges amongst business leaders and managers, which American advocates of Japanese economic revival believed would remove a significant proportion of Japan's skilled industrial élite. The cold warriors prevailed and in 1947–8 both *zaibatsu* dissolution and purges of businessmen were quietly wound down. In fact, in the first three years of the occupation, there had been a tentative revival in production, supported by SCAP aid and by preferential government loans to designated basic industries, such as coal and steel, by the Japanese government. None the less, recovery was very slow and had been seriously hindered by inflation.

The Dodge Line

Rampant inflation was one of the most serious economic problems during the occupation. In 1945 the rate of inflation had been 365 per cent. By 1948, various attempts at deflation had only managed to reduce price rises to 165 per cent (Tsuru, 1993). During 1948 a number of factors came together to produce a radical approach to Japan's monetary predicament. In Washington, where minds were being concentrated by the probability of communist victory in China, the National Security Council sponsored a policy of economic recovery in Japan as a bulwark against a future communist China. In Japan, the establishment of the second Yoshida cabinet in October 1948, with the financially orthodox Ikeda Hayato as minister of finance, helped create an atmosphere conducive to serious monetary reform. Unusually, President Truman took an active part in policy-making for Japan, and on 10 December 1948 he appointed Joseph Dodge as special emissary to oversee the Japanese economy.

Dodge, a Detroit banker, had been centrally involved in currency reforms in the western zones of Germany that had successfully curbed inflation and he was charged with the same objective in Japan. The thrust of Dodge's policies was to force a balanced budget upon the Japanese government, to cut off excess money supply by suspending loans from the Bank of Reconstruction and to end government subsidies to industry. As one dubious Japanese commentator on the Dodge Line has observed, 'it was only the authority of the Occupation forces that made its implementation possible' (Nakamura, 1981). Certainly, it was a dose of severe medicine for the Japanese economy, and the Yoshida cabinet agreed to it only because they could ultimately blame its repercussions on SCAP. Some observers have cast doubt upon the need for the Dodge Line whilst others have concluded that Dodge's policies laid the basis of Japan's future economic growth. Even with the Dodge Line, and earlier attempts to revive the Japanese economy, in 1950 Japan had neither a 'functioning competitive market' nor foreign currency reserves with which to buy machinery and raw materials. Essentially, the economy decisively revived only with the outbreak of the Korean War.

Rearmament and the Peace Treaty

The surest sign that US policy towards Japan was changing was rapid progress towards ending the occupation and the 180-degree turn on Japanese rearmament. In 1945, there had been no fixed idea on how long the occupation would last, but there was speculation that it might be as long as twenty-five years. As early as March 1947 General MacArthur had raised the possibility of bringing the occupation to an end by concluding a peace treaty with Japan, rather disingenuously claiming that the basic objectives of the occupation had been accomplished. It was argued that a peace treaty would not only return Japan to independence but also relieve the US of much of the financial burden of the occupation. Neither policy-makers in Washington nor the other Allies were ready to end the occupation in 1947 but the unfolding Cold War helped to change minds. The need to contain the Soviet Union and to strengthen the US security structure in the Pacific and elsewhere came to override other considerations. By 1949 State Department officials were much more receptive to the idea of a peace treaty. The Korean War was the final stimulus to a Japanese peace treaty. A peace conference was held in San Francisco in September 1951, although neither the Soviet Union nor China was present, and a peace treaty was signed on 8 September. The treaty promised the return of Japanese independence, although Okinawa continued under US control until 1972. The Soviet Union retained the Kurile Islands, north-east of Hokkaido and this remained a serious irritant in Japanese–Soviet relations.

Within hours of the peace treaty being signed, the Japanese paid the bill for it. A US–Japan Security Treaty tied Japan into the US security system, guaranteeing the Americans their military bases in Japan. The Security Treaty, which aroused ferocious opposition in Japan, raised the question of rearmament. Both MacArthur and Yoshida were to varying degrees opposed to Japanese rearmament; however, in the immediate aftermath of the outbreak of the Korean War in July 1950, SCAP created the 75,000-strong National Police Reserve, which, despite its name, was a military force. The National Police Reserve was the forerunner of Japan's re-emergence as a military power, despite article IX of the constitution. In July 1952 the National Police Reserve was converted into the Self-Defence Force, 146,000 strong, and post-occupation Japan steadily built formidable military power (Emmerson, 1971).

The occupation officially ended on 28 April 1952, although MacArthur had departed to fight the war in Korea in the summer of 1950 and real SCAP intervention in Japanese affairs had become less intrusive and had steadily wound down after 1947. The occupation had been remarkably smooth. The Americans had acted on the whole with great sensitivity. They had touched and significantly changed many of Japan's institutions. Some of the most important occupation reforms remain virtually intact after nearly fifty years. Most notably, of course, the 1947 constitution remains unamended, although this is as much a tribute to the mechanisms the Americans wrote into the constitution to obstruct fundamental constitutional change as it is to the Japanese people's attachment to the foreign-imposed document. Land reform and education changes were significant contributors to the relative social tranquillity and enormous economic development that Japan enjoyed after 1952. Even in areas where the occupation did not achieve its basic objectives, its impact was important. For instance, although SCAP failed to dissolve the *zaibatsu*, they did sufficiently disrupt ownership and management to allow younger, more dynamic managers to gain influence, which was to be vital to the rapid growth of the Japanese economy in the 1950s, 1960s and early 1970s. Practically, the largest contribution which the occupation made was, quite literally, to keep millions of Japanese alive. After 28 April 1952, the Japanese were once again masters of their own destiny.

3

THE QUEST FOR POLITICAL STABILITY AND ECONOMIC GROWTH, 1952–60

SCAP had exercised little real direction since the late 1940s and the San Francisco peace treaty did little more than formally recognise the reality of Japanese independence. The Yoshida government, which negotiated the treaty, had effectively ruled Japan since 1948, and would continue to govern until Yoshida was forced from office at the end of 1954. The US–Japan Security Treaty, which the Americans had imposed as a condition for the peace treaty imposed by the United States, tied Japan into the US security system. In Japan, the Security Treaty was widely perceived as an 'unequal treaty', which, like those of the nineteenth century, had been forced upon a helpless nation. It did not materially alter the position or stance of Japan in the Cold War. Restoring Japan's sovereignty in itself made no real difference to the economy but the outbreak of the Korean War in June 1950, coupled with the financial stability which the Dodge Line had imposed, inaugurated a period of rapid industrial development. This was the beginning of the post-war economic 'miracle'.

The Political Dominance of Yoshida Shigeru

Yoshida Shigeru, the dominant figure in Japanese politics

between 1948 and 1954, had become a party leader by ac-
cident. He had been a foreign ministry bureaucrat and had
served as Japanese ambassador to Britain between 1936 and
1938. This would have made him a prime candidate for
purge after the war had he not avoided serious political involvement after 1938 and also in 1944 been imprisoned for
a month by the wartime authorities. To SCAP, this washed
away the taint of his prewar service and he was thus free to
take up the leadership of the Liberal Party in May 1946,
when the first choice, Hatoyama Ichirō, was suddenly
purged. Yoshida was conservative, bordering on the reactionary, and senior figures in the occupation liked neither
him nor his ideas and held no high opinion of his leadership qualities. His background and personal demeanour did
not really suit him to be a politician but he was, none the
less, the leading figure in Japan's political scene during a
crucial period. Yoshida played a central role in charting
Japan's responses to the occupation and he was the single
most important force in trying to reverse some of the occupation reforms. To most Japanese, he is the best known,
although not the most popular, figure in postwar Japanese
politics (Dower, 1979).

Both SCAP and Washington had been reluctant to see
Yoshida become prime minister following the fall of the
Ashida coalition cabinet in 1948. There was no choice other
than Yoshida since the Katayama and Ashida cabinets had
demonstrated the catastrophic failure of coalition politics.
Yoshida's grip on office was not firm until his Democratic
Liberal Party won a decisive victory in the general election
held in January 1949. This marked the symbolic inception
of conservative political hegemony in post-independent
Japan. In the late 1940s and early 1950s Yoshida did not
simply create the tradition of victory for conservative parties. He spawned two fundamental facets of Japanese
conservative politics which have profoundly affected the
nation's politics since 1950. Yoshida pioneered the flow of
former bureaucrats into the ruling conservative parties and

71

he also started the construction of personal factions within conservative politics (Dower, 1979).

The Democratic Liberal Party which emerged victorious in 1949 was essentially one that represented business: 61 per cent of Democratic Liberals elected to the House of Representatives were businessmen. Significantly, 17 per cent of those representatives were former bureaucrats, pioneer builders of the bridge between the professional senior civil service, government, politics and big business. As a distinguished ex-bureaucrat himself, Yoshida was naturally disposed towards these former bureaucrat politicians. The modern Japanese bureaucracy had amassed immense prestige since its creation following the Meiji restoration and participation of senior civil servants in cabinets before 1945 reinforced the tradition of bureaucratic involvement in government. Yoshida had good reason to entice and favour ex-bureaucrats into politics. In the early postwar years, the bureaucracy was the only significant prewar élite group not extensively purged by SCAP, partly because senior civil servants were indispensable in implementing the occupation reforms. Former bureaucrats who entered politics were a valuable and attractive reservoir of undoubted ability and they rapidly became an important source of ministerial talent for Yoshida; seven of them passed from being newly elected members of parliament straight into ministerial office. These bureaucratic conservative parliamentarians were to be one of the principal sources of the distinctive personal factions which came to characterise conservative politics. Amongst the ex-bureaucrat protégés of Yoshida who were elected in January 1949 were Ikeda Hayato and Satō Eisaku, who would inherit and use the personal following that Yoshida developed to dominate Japanese politics as prime ministers between 1960 and 1972, the period of maximum economic growth (Tomita et al., 1986).

Factionalism became pervasive in the successor to the conservative parties of the early 1950s, the Liberal Democratic Party, only after 1956 and reached full maturity only in the 1970s, but none the less Yoshida did begin the process, creating a personal following that numbered around 140 by 1952. Yoshida had never been personally popular in the Democratic Liberal Party, so in 1948–9 he set about bolstering his leadership by creating his own personal support base within the party. The bulk of this so-called 'Yoshida School' was drawn from the new blood flowing into conservative politics at the end of the 1940s. A disproportionate number of the Yoshida faction were former civil servants attracted into politics by the prime minister himself. In the 1950s and 1960s factions dominated by former bureaucrats would wield unusual influence in the ruling party.

The forces at work on Yoshida in the late 1940s and 1950s were complex. Yoshida liked to believe that he had raised pragmatism and realism to an art form. He had convinced himself that Japan would have to buy its independence by signing the Security Treaty and agreeing to become a cornerstone of the US security system in the western Pacific. Yet, as a genuine conservative, he had been aghast at the extent and scale of some of the early occupation reforms. By 1951, before the formal conclusion of the San Francisco peace treaty, Yoshida was promoting a 'rectification-of-excesses' campaign to reverse some of the changes SCAP had imposed. In one important sphere, however, Yoshida did not believe that the occupation reforms had been excessive. He was a much less enthusiastic exponent of Japan's rearmament than most other conservative politicians. Yoshida felt that rearmament would be both politically and economically onerous for Japan and he held off pressure for remilitarisation from both fellow conservative politicians and from the United States. Naturally, this brought him into conflict with both over the issue, although experience showed that the rhetoric of many conservatives was not matched by their zeal in rearming Japan when their opportunities came.

Another complication that Yoshida faced during his tenure of office was the 'depurging' in 1952 of those politicians who had been excluded from politics by SCAP. This released into the conservative political arena a group of prewar and wartime politicians and other notables who regarded the new postwar politicians as interlopers. They resented the political status gained by those who had entered politics after 1945 and whose advancement had been largely the result of their own forced exclusion from politics. In particular, these professional politicians took exception to ex-bureaucrats rising to prominence in conservative politics. Naturally, greatest resentment was reserved for the arch-symbol of these new ex-bureaucrat politicians, Yoshida Shigeru. This animosity was personified by the extremely sour relationship between Yoshida and Hatoyama Ichirō, whose purging had given the Liberal Party leadership to Yoshida in 1946. In their assaults on the prime minister and his supporters the returnees' appealed to Japanese nationalist sentiments. They argued that by signing the Security Treaty with the United States Yoshida had reduced Japan to the status of 'subordinate independence'. Further, although Yoshida had presided over the creation of postwar Japan's armed forces, firstly when the National Police Reserve as set up in 1950 and then when it was transformed into the Self-Defence Force in July 1952, he was a reluctant rearmer and this gave his detractors more nationalist ammunition. In addition, Yoshida and his three cabinets in office between February 1949 and December 1954 had a very complex set of economic and social problems to address. The effects of the Dodge Line had been unpopular in Japan and the government had to dampen down continuing popular unrest over poor living standards.

Political tensions built up relatively slowly. For three years after his victory in the 1949 election, Yoshida was spared internal opposition in his party but the return of the purgees to political life in 1952 planted the seeds of internal dissent. Opposition to Yoshida crystallised around Hatoyama, who claimed that Yoshida had agreed he would be leader of the Liberal Party only so long as Hatoyama was excluded from politics. Hatoyama was therefore mortified when Yoshida refused to relinquish the premiership in his favour in 1952. Yoshida's high-handed and insensitive attitude towards other depurged notables, such as Kishi Nobusuke, who would become prime minister in 1957, alienated other influential figures. The political environment was complicated by personal factors. Kishi and Yoshida, who were very distantly related, disliked each other, but Satō Eisaku, one of Yoshida's principal lieutenants, was Kishi's natural brother. To a large extent, the feuding within conservative ranks set the new postwar politicians, of whom Yoshida was the foremost example, against the traditional party politicians who had been active before and during the war. In addition to the serious difficulties which Yoshida and his supporters had from Hatoyama and the returnees, the prime minister had to take responsibility for poor election results in October 1952 and March 1953 which raised the spectre of the Socialist Party being swept into office in the near future. Then, his government became engulfed in a scandal concerning subsidies to shipbuilding yards (Kurzman, 1960).

In April 1954 Satō Eisaku, then secretary-general of Yoshida's Liberal Party, was accused of complicity in the shipbuilding scandal and a warrant issued for his arrest. Yoshida used his authority as prime minister to postpone Satō's arrest and thereby keep his cabinet in office. Yoshida had acted legally, but his actions provoked a storm of opposition and seriously undermined his authority. His public popularity was in steep decline, his conservative enemies were closing in upon him and his position was becoming untenable. Pressure from business interests worried by the possibility of a socialist government had led Hatoyama temporarily to reconcile his differences with Yoshida. Taking advantage of the blizzard of unpopularity that was engulfing Yoshida, Hatoyama ostentatiously left the Liberal Party on 24 November 1954 and allied with the conservative Progressive Party to create a new conservative grouping, the Democratic Party. Yoshida's other enemies within the Liberal Party now turned upon him. Faced with a no-confidence motion in parliament, Yoshida's cabinet resigned. Yoshida was now virtually isolated within his own party. On 7 December 1954 the man who had been prime minister for seven of the nine years following the surrender bowed to the inevitable and resigned (Kosaka, 1972).

The Creation of the Liberal Democratic Party

Within a year of the fall of Yoshida, the two existing conservative parties had coalesced to create a single conservative party which was to monopolise political power for nearly four decades. The disappearance of Yoshida helped to create a united conservative party in two ways. Firstly, some of the obstacles to closer relations between various groups and individuals in conservative politics were removed. Secondly, the departure of Yoshida stimulated the two wings of the Japan Socialist Party, which had split in 1951 over the Security Treaty question, to sink their differences and reunite. The re-emergence of a united Socialist Party, following so soon after their excellent election showing in March 1953, caused tremors throughout conservative political circles and, more importantly, among their financial supporters in big business.

In the 1950s, big business was the only significant source of funds for the conservative parties. Obviously, private companies used their money to create a political environment conducive to their interests. Big business had been deeply troubled by the political implications of the antagonism between Yoshida and Hatoyama. After Yoshida's departure, the paymasters began to exert pressure for a united conservative front to block the election of a socialist government. Until January 1955 there had been four organs of big business channelling funds to the various conservative parties but, a month after the fall of Yoshida, big business centralised its political funding and used its money to pressure the conservative politicians to unite. Feelers were put out and these resulted in cautious talks between the two parties, using the good offices of the owner of the *Yomiuri* newspaper and, significantly, a senior official of the

Japan Chamber of Commerce. The negotiations and formal contacts broadened out until a joint Liberal Party–Democratic Party conference held at Chūō University in Tokyo on 15 November 1955 formally launched the unified, conservative Liberal Democratic Party (Thayer, 1969). The LDP was very much the creation of big business which had forced the right-wing politicians to sink their differences and use their energies to fight the socialists (Tomita *et al.*, 1986). In October 1955 the two wings of the Japan Socialist Party had reunited to form a single party. With the founding of the LDP Japan acquired a two-party political system.

It was hardly surprising that the foundation of the united conservative party was closely followed by the rapid development of divisive factionalism within that party. The earliest pattern of factionalism in the LDP was simply a reflection of the origins of the party; four of the eight identifiable factions had their origins in the Liberal Party and four in the Democratic Party. The early factional geography of the LDP revealed a trend for some factions to attract ex-bureaucrats whilst others appealed to professional politicians. In 1955–6 three of the eight factions were preponderantly ex-bureaucrat whilst the other five tended to represent non-bureaucrat politicians. In 1956 the LDP introduced elections for the presidency of the LDP, a post that automatically brought with it the premiership, and this accelerated the growth and consolidation of factionalism within the party. It also promoted the so-called 'money politics', an essential feature of LDP factionalism. During the 1956 presidential election, the faction of Kishi Nobusuke, the unsuccessful candidate for office, spent over ¥300 million, whilst the successful Ishibashi Tanzan faction spent ¥150 million. Between 1956 and 1960, when Kishi Nobusuke was prime minister, factionalism became firmly entrenched. Kishi was one of the earliest cynical wielders of factional power and it was poetic justice when he fell from office in 1960 partly because of the defection of two of the factions with which he had formed a tactical alliance. Faction and money politics sustained the LDP's monopoly of office for thirty-eight years, but was also substantially responsible for the end of that monopoly in the summer of 1993 (Tomita *et al.*, 1986).

From the start, factions within the LDP were the personal following of a particular politician and rarely mirrored any serious political or ideological opinion. Postwar conservative politics developed an insatiable appetite for money and one role of the leader was to provide these financial resources. A vital function of the faction leader was to ensure that each of his followers enjoyed some ministerial office and served on those parliamentary committees that could visibly channel patronage to their constituencies. In return for this financial largesse and career preferment, the faction leader received his followers' electoral support in the elections and labyrinthine politicking within the LDP. These factions negotiated and combined with each other, and these swirling eddies of factional interaction became one of the principal arenas of postwar Japanese politics (Stockwin, 1988).

Factionalism in the LDP has received heavy and largely justified criticism. The factions are the main reason for the growth of 'money politics' and corruption in the political system of postwar Japan. Factionalism has been attacked for the way in which it reduced the authority of political leaders, and especially that of the prime minister. Further, incessant factional infighting, combined with a weakened party and government leadership, complicated and slowed decision making and diluted the input of politicians to policy formation, to the advantage of the role and influence of the bureaucracy. On the other hand, an exclusively negative assessment of LDP factionalism would provide a skewed picture of postwar Japanese politics. So long as they existed factions were a fundamental obstacle to the emergence of dictatorial power in what was, in reality, a one-party state between 1955 and 1993. In addition, the interplay between factions did provide policy alternatives which added to the flexibility of LDP governments, especially in the 1970s and 1980s. In any case, given the prevalence of factions in most

Japanese institutions, their development in the LDP was almost inevitable (Baerwald, 1986).

The Polarization of Politics, 1954–60

In December 1954 Hatoyama achieved his most cherished ambition when he succeeded Yoshida as prime minister. Hatoyama began his premiership as leader of the Democratic Party, which was to the right of Yoshida's Liberal Party. Ironically, his government was initially sustained in office by the JSP, which had extracted a promise of an early general election that the socialists hoped to win. Hatoyama, who was personally very popular, and his Democratic Party won a working majority in the election held in February 1955. Whilst he was prime minister, the Liberal and Democratic Parties came together to form an electorally powerful conservative bloc and Hatoyama was also able to achieve his aim of normalising relations with the Soviet Union, thereby clearing the last obstacle to Japan's entry into the United Nations, just as he left office in December 1956. Domestically Hatoyama was much less successful. He had prevented a socialist election victory but, as a conservative, he also wished to reverse some of the occupation reforms. In this sphere his achievements were very limited.

Between 1951 and 1954 the Yoshida government had taken considerable strides in recentralising the police force, control over which SCAP had passed to local authorities. In 1956, Hatoyama rammed the Local Education Law through parliament, a measure that began the reassertion of central control over the education system. Hatoyama's main objective, however, was to amend the constitution; as a nationalist, his particular target was article IX which constitutionally disarmed Japan. To accomplish this Hatoyama needed a two-thirds majority in parliament. Hatoyama's grand strategy for constitutional reform was to change the electoral system used for the House of Representatives from multi-member to single-member constituencies. Such a change in the electoral system would undoubtedly have damaged the electoral prospects of the opposition and could have yielded a two-thirds parliamentary majority for the new Liberal Democratic Party. Naturally Hatoyama's strategy was fiercely resisted by the JSP but Hatoyama's electoral reform plans foundered not on the rock of socialist opposition but because the anti-Hatoyama factions in the new LDP feared that electoral reform would damage their influence and strengthen rival factions. These anti-Hatoyama factions colluded with the JSP and blocked electoral reform. Hatoyama was not politically strong enough to survive the failure of his grand schemes and he resigned in December 1956.

Hatoyama was succeeded as prime minister by Ishibashi Tanzan but serious illness forced him to resign two months later. Kishi Nobusuke, the defeated candidate in the party's presidential election, became prime minister in February 1957. Kishi's succession to the prime ministership led to a rapid polarisation in Japanese politics. In part, this was a consequence of Kishi's character, beliefs and past. Kishi never lost that arrogant disdain for the public which often afflicted former bureaucrats, and he projected the image of a haughty bureaucrat rather than of a populist politician. He carried some heavy historical baggage which seriously tarnished his image. He had been a senior Japanese bureaucrat in Manchukuo, had held the key post of minister of commerce and industry in the Tōjō government, and during the war he had been minister of munitions. After the surrender, Kishi had been arrested and imprisoned by SCAP. Although indicted as a class-A war criminal he had never been tried. Kishi had staunch nationalist and anti-communist views. Kishi was detested by left-wingers who naturally concentrated their fire on a past which laid him open to accusations of working to reverse the democratic ground gained during the occupation, and of trying to put the clock back to pre-1945. In fact, Kishi's views and policies were complex. In some ways, he resembled the Meiji oligarchs. Just as they were anxious to have Japan accepted as an equal to the western powers, so Kishi was anxious to reassert Japan's place in the world and to boost Japan's international prestige. Like the Meiji leaders, Kishi believed that Japan could gain international acceptance by developing its social, political and economic institutions until they closely resembled those of Europe and North America. Kishi maintained that the government should have a key role in directing the economy and stimulating economic growth, which would not only enhance the prosperity of the Japanese people but also improve Japan's international image. Although a conservative, Kishi was willing to sponsor a system of social welfare to secure the approval of the outside world, and his government laid the foundations of Japan's welfare structure (Kosaka, 1972).

Kishi's parliamentary methods were confrontational and this ultimately proved his undoing. He used the LDP's parliamentary majority to force through a rating system for teachers and provoked confrontation with the teacher's union. In the face of determined JSP opposition, Kishi tried to push through a radical increase in the power of the police. The socialists adopted the classic Japanese parliamentary tactic of boycotting the Diet and that, combined with mass demonstrations against the revised police law, forced Kishi to abandon the measure. Clashes over the teachers and the revised police law dangerously polarised Japanese politics, stimulating the growth of mass organisations which the socialists and the communists tried to take over. Kishi's nemesis was not, however, the result of purely domestic issues but rather the consequence of emotions unleashed by the revision of the US–Japanese Security Treaty. The original Security Treaty had been signed five hours after the San Francisco peace treaty and was not popular in Japan. The left opposed it because it tied Japan to the United States, whilst the right argued that it was no more than the occupation by other means since it placed constraints both on Japan's sovereignty and its ability to conduct an independent foreign policy. During 1958–9 the Kishi government successfully negotiated a revision of the treaty which was much more favourable to Japan than the original treaty. The Security Treaty itself was opposed by the JSP, the Communist Party and by a substantial segment of public opinion. In parliamentary committees, the JSP skilfully obstructed the ratification of the revised treaty for nearly a year (Kosaka, 1972).

Kishi was anxious to have the treaty revision accepted before a visit to Japan by President Eisenhower, scheduled for 19 June 1960. On 19 May the JSP refused to extend the parliamentary session to allow passage of the treaty. Kishi responded by using a variety of strategems to force through the treaty in the early hours of 20 May. Kishi's customary high-handed parliamentary tactics provoked an unprecedented storm of demonstrations. On 10 June 1960 Eisenhower's press secretary, James Haggarty, had to be rescued by helicopter when he attempted to get from Haneda Airport to the centre of Tokyo. On 15 June 1960 the disturbances reached a crescendo when radical students stormed the parliamentary compound; a student was killed in the subsequent fierce battle with the riot police. The situation was so dangerous that next day Eisenhower's visit was postponed. The new Security Treaty became law on 19 June, accompanied by a statement from Kishi that he would resign once the revision issue was settled, a promise he honoured on 18 July 1960.

The 1960 Security Treaty disturbances were the most serious domestic political crisis in Japan since the end of the occupation. Whilst there had been no chance of the government being overthrown by force, social order had been severely buffetted by serious, potentially dangerous, civil and industrial strife. Within the LDP, the media and public opinion, much of the blame for the crisis was laid at the door of the high-handed, arrogant personality and tactics of Kishi. Henceforth, the LDP would take care to avoid abusing their apparently permanent parliamentary majority and this helped to curb popular distaste for the party's monopoly of power.

The Problems of the Opposition

The formation of the LDP in November 1955 had produced a two-party system in Japan. This pattern barely survived the decade and by 1960 Japan had four significant political parties. In part, this was the result of a revival in the Japan Communist Party's fortunes, but it stemmed largely from internal strife and disruption within the JSP and the defection of moderates from it. The Japan Socialist Party, founded in November 1945, was an amalgamation of a number of rival socialist movements which had existed in the 1920s and 1930s, hence 'its founders came bearing miscellaneous intellectual baggage from the prewar period' (Stockwin, 1986: 86). Electorally, the JSP did well after the surrender and in June 1947 the leader of the party, Katayama Tetsu, became the prime minister of a coalition government. That government was a disaster which stimulated fierce infighting between the two main wings of the party. The socialist element in the Katayama cabinet had been largely drawn from the right wing of the party. The fall of the Katayama cabinet in February 1948 was caused, in part, by members of parliament belonging to the left of the JSP voting against the budget of the coalition government whose leader was also the leader of their party. Twice in 1948 the JSP split temporarily into right- and left-wing sub-parties. In January 1950 the JSP even managed to split into three. Then, in October 1951, a dispute over whether to support the peace treaty led to a decisive split into two parties, both of which confusingly called themselves the Japan Socialist Party. The left-wing version of the JSP steadily gained support over the right-JSP. Partly this was because the latter was tarred with responsibility for the failure of the coalition governments in 1947–8. Mainly it was due to the financial and organisational backing that the left wing received from the powerful Sōhyō trade union federation, itself increasingly controlled by left-wingers. This enabled the left-JSP to boost its electoral support well ahead of the right-wing variant of the party.

The two versions of the JSP did well electorally in the mid-1950s. Their success was based on support for such popular concerns as opposition to constitutional revision and rearmament and general resistance to attempts by conservative governments to reverse occupation reform. In October 1955 the two JSPs came together to form one party again because of the real prospect of a socialist victory in the next general election. The electoral danger from a re-unified JSP was the immediate stimulus for the creation of a single conservative party, the LDP, in November 1955 and during the remainder of the decade the JSP was unable to break through electorally. This bred frustration in the frenetic, polarised political environment provoked by the increasingly strident revisionist policies and high-handed tactics of the Kishi government. Within the party, the left gained ascendancy over the more moderate elements in part because of growing organisational dependence on the left-wing-dominated Sōhyō and also because of the machinations of an intellectual pressure group, *Shakaishugi Kyōkai*, which rejected the possibility of socialism coming through democratic, parliamentary means. Ostensibly these splits in the socialist edifice revolved around disagreements about renewal of the US–Japanese Security Treaty. In reality, the JSP was being riven apart by deep ideological differences between the various factions. In October 1959 Nishio Suehiro, the leader of the more moderate tendency within the JSP, led a defection of some of his supporters from the party. In January 1960 the defectors formed the Democratic Socialist Party (*Minshu Shakaitō*), permanently splitting postwar Japan's already fissiparous socialist movement (Stockwin, 1986). Japan no longer had a two-party system. By 1960 it was little more than a one-and-a-half party system; it would soon become a multi-party system.

Building the Foundations for High-Speed Growth

The most spectacular change in Japan in the thirty years following the Second World War took place in the economy. Between 1946, when the economy was almost at rock bottom, and 1976 the Japanese economy grew fifty-five fold. Between 1951 and 1960 the size of Japan's national income more than doubled, whilst per capita gross national product trebled. In turn, between 1960 and 1973 national income more than trebled. In the 1950s, industry accounted for only one-quarter of Japan's gross national product, but two decades later this had increased to 45 per cent. Between 1953 and 1971 output in manufacturing industry increased on average by 14 per cent per annum, compared with an average 8.8 per cent rise in the national income. In twenty years Japan achieved a level of industrialisation within its economy that it took Britain and Germany fifty years, and Italy hundred years, to achieve (Boltho, 1975). This rapid economic growth was accompanied by rapid structural change in the economy. Agriculture rapidly declined in relative importance, whilst within the industrial sector there were significant changes in the nature and relative shares of particular industries. The enormous dimensions of Japan's economic growth since 1950 are beyond dispute. Endless controversy surrounds the factors that produced and sustained the postwar economic 'miracle'.

The Japanese economy had been seriously disrupted by the Second World War but it did contain seeds which would contribute to growth. Firstly, during the war Japan had not been invaded or become the scene of all-destructive land battles. The country had escaped division during the occupation and was spared the economic dislocation that occurred in Germany. After 1945 there was none of the destructive and violent internal conflict that many of Japan's east and south-east Asian neighbours suffered. Finally, the toll of war on Japan's managers and skilled workers had been relatively small, preserving much of prewar Japan's skilled human capital. These advantages were complemented by certain occupation policies. One vital contribution by the Americans during the occupation years was the supply of raw materials and other vital resources.

This helped prime limited resumption of industrial activity in the immediate postwar economic trough. The occupation also contributed to economic revival by enforcing a series of anti-inflationary measures, culminating in the Dodge Line of 1949, which stabilised the yen. Industrial recovery would have been endangered had Japan's financial system remained unstable. On the negative side, Japan's industrial economy was severely handicapped by a vicious circle in industrial production. Coal was needed to make steel, and steel required to make the machinery necessary to mine coal – but both were in short supply. This barrier to industrial growth was only slowly brought down by substantial US imports of oil into occupied Japan in the late 1940s. Generally, Japanese manufacturing industry was fed by raw materials supplied by the United States. By 1949–50 some significant sectors of the economy had begun to revive, although foreign trade was still stagnant (Johnson, 1986). Gradual economic recovery was transformed into a boom by an fortuitous event outside Japan.

The Korean War and the Economy

Until 1950 the government had tried to resuscitate Japanese industry by using 'priority production' methods which targeted the coal and steel industries. These policies had partially revived basic industries but the financial radicalism of the Dodge Line of 1949 had shaken industrial growth. In 1950 the Japanese economy was again stagnant. The Korean War altered this. Yoshida Shigeru described the Korean War, which broke out in June 1950 and continued until July 1953, as 'a gift of the gods'. It was the most important single factor in reviving the flagging Japanese economy. Japan became a vital source of supplies for the US forces fighting in Korea. 'Special procurements', the means by which Americans bought Japanese goods and services for valuable dollars, contributed $930 million to the Japanese economy between 1950 and 1953. It was not only basic industries such as iron and steel which received a powerful boost. Profits made in repairing US military vehicles during the Korean War was the first real stimulus to Japan's postwar automobile industry (Tsuru, 1993). When the peace treaty was signed in 1952 the Korean War had helped to raise industrial production to a level some 15 per cent above the average in 1934–6 (the peak of prewar production), although it did not attain the levels reached in wartime until 1955. The effect of the Korean War on Japan's international economic position was enormously important. Between 1949 and 1951 the value of Japan's exports increased from $500 million to $1250 million. The expansion of Japan's international trade built up Japanese foreign exchange reserves, which were used to import the latest industrial technology from abroad. Without this foreign technology there could have been no high-speed growth in the 1950s and 1960s (Denison and Chung, 1976).

The opportunities the Korean War offered to Japanese industry led to a change of direction. Government policy shifted to industrial rationalisation aimed at modernising basic industries, especially steel and coal. This would reduce costs and make Japan internationally more competitive. Between 1951 and 1954 it was planned to channel investment capital amounting to ¥63 billion through the banks into the iron and steel industry. In the event, over ¥120 billion was invested. Combinations of supporting industries and technologies were sited in the most geographically advantageous positions, developing into vast and efficient industrial parks (Uchino, 1983). In 1953 rationalisation was put into practice when the Kawasaki Steel Company opened its integrated rolling strip mill in Chiba prefecture, giving Japan the world's most advanced steelmaking facility. A second government steel rationalisation plan poured a further ¥500 billion into Japan's steel industry This stimulated the building of more integrated steel mills around the coasts, using the latest imported steelmaking technology. Much of this investment was demand-led, responding to an explosion in the need for high-quality steel for the growing shipbuilding, automobile and domestic appliance industries. By the end of the 1950s, only a decade after it had emerged prostrate from the war, Japan's steel industry was second only to that of the United States (Kosai, 1988).

Rationalising the coal industry was much less successful. Geology made Japan's coal difficult to mine and its quality was poor. In addition, the coal industry's prospects were seriously damaged by industrial strife. A miners' strike in the autumn of 1952 led manufacturers to began a sustained search for alternative sources of energy. Throughout the remainder of the decade energy users steadily switched from coal to oil and electricity. This move from coal to oil by Japan's manufacturers and generators of electricity was stimulated both by the low world price of oil and also by the emergence of the supertanker, which led to a rapid decline in the costs of transporting oil from newly developed fields in the Middle East to Japan. As oil became increasingly important to the Japanese economy, the government tried to stem the tide of this movement from coal to imported oil. It was quite unable to do so, demonstrating the limits to government control over the economy. Plentiful and cheap supplies of oil were crucial to the rapid growth of Japan's industrial economy, but it did make the country extremely dependent on foreign oil and this would have serious economic consequences in 1973 and 1979 (Nakamura, 1981).

Other industries developed in the 1950s. In 1935 Japan had been the world's third largest shipbuilder, constructing 11 per cent of the world's total. Most of Japan's shipyards had survived the war intact but during the occupation there was little serious activity. As in other sectors, the Korean War stimulated shipbuilding. From 1951 the government-controlled Japan Development Bank injected serious investment capital into the industry. Growing world demand for oil produced an insatiable demand for ever larger tankers, a trend accelerated by the closing of the Suez Canal in 1956, which increased the cost of shipping oil from the Middle East to Europe and North America. The Japanese shipbuilding industry strove successfully to satisfy this demand. New technology was brought in, particularly the welding of prefabricated sections. The great supertankers were the basis upon which Japan became the world's largest shipbuilding nation by 1960, producing around 20 per cent of world tonnage. Demand from this burgeoning shipbuilding industry was a significant factor in the revival and growth of the steel industry (Denison and Chung, 1976).

The development of iron and steel was accompanied by, indeed partly the result of, the growth of other industries, especially the manufacture of domestic appliances and the early development of the Japanese automobile industry. Between 1953 and 1956 the production of washing machines increased eightfold. In 1956 1 per cent of Japanese households had a television set; by 1960 half of all Japanese families owned a television. This explosion in the production of television sets and other electrical consumer goods was achieved by the emerging giants of Japanese electronics, such as Matsushita and Hitachi. Although the Korean War had given Japanese vehicle manufacturing a boost, the great expansion of the automobile industry only came after 1960. None the less, in the 1950s Nissan, Toyota, Isuzu and Hino not only produced cars and commercial vehicles under license from the west but they also began to produce Japanese designed and engineered trucks and cars.

In the decade following the occupation Japan experienced the so-called 'management science boom', during the course of which many of the management and production methods that characterised Japan's rapid growth were introduced into large-scale industrial enterprises. The United States was the source of many of these managerial and organisational innovations. During the 1950s, and into the 1960s, Japanese managers adopted and built upon the theoretical work of American quality control experts, most notably W. Edwards Deming, to create the institution of 'quality circles'. In 1957 the concept of 'total quality control' was introduced into Japan (Fruin, 1992). These practices, widely held to be responsible for the consistent high quality of Japanese manufactured goods, spread rapidly through large-scale industry. Quality became an obsession in Japanese manufacturing industry during the 1950s and early 1960s because Japan's straitened international economic position demanded that there be no waste of valuable imported machinery or raw materials. Thus, Japanese industry put far more effort into quality control than their international competitors. Japanese manufacturers were also searching for innovations in logistics and production. In 1956 Toyota and its satellite companies introduced the 'just-in-time' (*kanban*) system. 'Just-in-time' required subcontractors to deliver components exactly when needed on the production line. This greatly reduced stocks of spares held in factories, cut the costs of warehousing and minimised the amount of money tied up in components. Quality control, quality circles and the just-in-time system became distinctive features of Japanese manufacturing tactics, and were widely adopted elsewhere – including the United States (McMillan, 1985).

The Government and Economic Growth

One of the most hotly contested subjects in postwar Japanese history remains the relative contributions of government, bureaucracy, private enterprise and market forces to Japan's rapid economic growth. Naturally, government was committed to fostering expansion of the economy. Few doubt the significant contribution made by the high level of political stability provided by almost permanent conservative government. Government policies in areas such as education undoubtedly contributed vital support to rapid economic growth. Substantial controversy swirls around the extent to which the most successful economy in the postwar world acquired this status through official direction and planning. One distinguished scholar of postwar Japan has stated that the 'high-growth system was one of the most rational and productive industrial policies ever devised by any government', although conceding that 'its essential rationality was

not perceived until after it had already started producing results unprecedented for Japan or any other industrialized
economy' (Johnson, 1986: 199).

The counter-argument is that the role of the government
and its bureaucracy was marginal because government
largely implemented policies which the private sector had
no problem in accepting given that they were advantageous
to business. This school argues that big corporations simply
rejected governmental and bureaucratic 'administrative
guidance' that was not conducive to business interests:

> no amount of argument can show that the bureaucratic
> controls that [the civil service] exercised so extensively
> could have been a net disservice to economic growth. But
> neither does the fact that the economy grew rapidly un-
> der the bureaucrats make the case that official planning
> and direction did it.   (Tresize and Suzuki, 1976: 809)

Did the government and the bureaucracy, develop a series
of strategic plans for the industrial development of Japan,
what is often called 'industrial policy', and did they create
a set of tools to enable them tactically to implement those
industrial policies?

After 1868 the Meiji government had tried to develop the
means to guide the economy. These had only been of limited
effectiveness. New legislation to control the development of
the economy passed in the 1930s was also less effective than
intended. After the war, the two principal instruments of
government and bureaucratic intervention in the economy
were the Ministry of Finance and the Ministry of International Trade and Industry (MITI). Both had their origins
before the Second World War, although MITI had started
life in 1925 as the Ministry of Commerce and Industry and
was only christened MITI in May 1949. The methods which
these, and lesser bureaucratic agencies, used to influence
the economy in the 1950s were both formal and informal.
The formal instruments which the government and bureaucracy manipulated were based upon economic controls

inherited from the occupation. Most importantly, the Japanese government was bequeathed control of Japan's foreign exchange. Politicians and bureaucrats decided which industries and companies could import raw materials and foreign technology by allocating Japan's scarce foreign currency. This device gave government and bureaucracy considerable influence over the nature and extent of industrial development in the 1950s.

The Yoshida government used measures inherited from the occupation to protect chosen sectors of the Japanese economy from foreign competition. Once Japan formally regained its sovereignty in April 1952 the government, advised by the economic bureaucracy, was able to grant tax concessions to those sectors of the economy that they wished to support and advance. In the early 1950s a new lever of influence was put in the hands of government and bureaucracy. During the Korean War boom, the growth of those Japanese industries responding to US demand was threatened by a lack of investment capital. To avoid this, MITI successfully lobbied for 'overloans'. These permitted the commercial banks to lend to selected firms far more money than their worth or immediate prospects would justify. The risk these 'overloans' represented to the commercial banks was covered by the central, government-controlled banking institutions, who acted as guarantors. Their role as insurer of 'overloans' gave the government and economic bureaucracy an added input into economic planning.

The less formal pressure which the government and bureaucracy tried to use was 'administrative guidance', which was not a consistent policy but a policy method. In essence, it used the great prestige and status of the bureaucracy in Japan, and the threat of using the government's levers of influence over the economy, to 'guide' the investment and other decisions of private companies. The effectiveness of 'administrative guidance' is debated, but it is reasonable to assume that circumstances in the 1950s gave the government and economic bureaucracy greater opportunities to influence the development and structure of the economy than in subsequent decades. According to the advocates of the government-orchestrated view of Japanese industrial growth in the 1950s and into the 1960s, the government, and especially the bureaucracy, used these 'overloans' and other levers to select and nurture various industries for growth as part of an overall plan for the industrial expansion of Japan. They used their various means to control the economy to limit the fierce competition which their policies might unleash (Johnson, 1986).

The International Economy and Japanese Economic Growth

The international economic environment that existed for nearly three decades following the end of the Second World War was of tremendous benefit to Japan. The Bretton Woods system, created in 1944, provided Japan with a stable international monetary system, which made decision-making on international economic matters relatively simple; whilst the General Agreement on Tariffs and Trade (GATT) built a postwar international trading system which was unprecedentedly open. Furthermore, this open international economic structure meant that Japan could import foreign technology relatively freely. Since Japan was a 'latecomer' in industrial development, and therefore its industrial growth was heavily dependent on the import of knowledge and plant from abroad, this was a key element for Japan even into the 1980s. The scale and importance of this import of foreign technology is demonstrated by its cost. Between 1945 and 1955 Japan spent $69 million on foreign technology, increasing to $281 million between 1956 and 1960, as high-speed growth began to take hold. This expanded to $684 million in the first five years of the 1960s and $1.54 billion between 1966 and 1970. In the final years of high-speed growth, $3.21 billion was spent on importing 10,789 items of foreign technology.

The most important phases of Japan's economic expansion occurred in a period of almost unprecedented world-wide economic growth and prosperity. This was no coincidence: Japan's growth was heavily dependent on growth world-wide and 'without this coincidence, Japan's economic growth would have taken a much longer and more hazardous path' (Inoguchi and Okimoto, 1988). Lastly, there is justice in the claim that Japan's economic growth was in part achieved by riding on the military coat-tails of the United States. Japan took advantage of the US position in the world to obtain access both to raw materials and to world markets whilst sheltering under the US military umbrella. A tiny percentage of Japanese national wealth, before the 1980s never more than 1 per cent, went on defence. The money saved could instead be invested in further industrial development; had Japan spend 6 or 7 per cent of GNP on the military, it would have reduced overall economic growth in the 1960s and early 1970s by up to 2 per cent per annum (Patrick and Rosovsky, 1976).

The Economy in the 1950s

The Japanese economy statistically recovered from the Second World War when in 1955 industrial output in Japan rose to exceed the maximum prewar levels. However, as one astute participant in Japan's postwar economic growth observes, 'Japan . . . still was small and relatively weak economically' (Kosai, 1986: 533). Growth had been rapid in the 1950s, and industries with considerable potential had been cultivated, although there was a restraint on the levels and smoothness of Japan's economic growth which continued until 1967. This 'balance of payments ceiling' was caused by growth sucking in substantial imports of raw materials and capital goods, which led to a serious deficit in the balance of payments. Governments dealt with this by imposing tight money policies through high interest rates and reduction in credit. This lowered domestic demand, the engine of Japanese economic growth, and thereby decelerated the economy. These monetary restraints could be slackened, for once the balance of payments approached equilibrium, the domestic economy would expand and growth would speed up. This happened in 1954, 1957, 1961 and 1963 when financial and monetary restraint in response to balance of payments problems slowed down economic growth (Nakamura, 1981).

Japan's first eight years of independence had been politically confusing but economically successful. The foundation of the LDP in November 1955 and the splits in the JSP in the late 1950s were the beginning of nearly forty years of LDP dominance – though this was not clear at the time. Japanese politics, and society, had seemed dangerously polarised by government policies and popular opposition to constitutional revision and the US–Japan Security Treaty. Economically, the first years of independence could be counted a success. Basic industries such as iron and steel had not only been revived but had become world leaders. New industries emerged and some of the distinctive features of Japanese production methods were already in place. The Japanese people had become much more prosperous. In 1954 consumption had reached the level of the best prewar years and by 1957 consumption was 27 per cent greater than in 1954. Increasingly, the Japanese consumer had the 'three electric treasures': a washing machine, a refrigerator and a television set.

4

BOOM TIME IN JAPAN: HIGH-SPEED GROWTH 1960–73

The years between 1960 and 1973 have the aura of a golden age for a Japan which was enjoying unprecedentedly high and sustained rates of economic growth. The official aim of doubling national income in a decade proved hopelessly conservative. Economic growth was accompanied by widespread and growing prosperity. More of the population came to perceive themselves as being middle class. In politics, the quiet premiership of the genial Ikeda Hayato from 1960 to 1964 calmed the frenetic, polarised and often violent political atmosphere that had enveloped the Kishi government and exploded into the 1960 Security Treaty crisis. The sense of political stability and tranquillity was boosted by the reassuring presence of Satō Eisaku, who succeeded Ikeda as prime minister in 1964 and would be Japan's longest-serving premier. The growing sense of achievement, well-being and optimism had its most spectacular manifestation in the highly successful Olympic Games held in Tokyo in 1964. This Olympiad symbolically marked Japan's return to world prominence. Towards the end of this 'golden age', however, economic, social and political developments began to shake this contentment. Like many other developed societies, Japan was convulsed by widespread and violent student rebellion in 1968. By 1970 popular disquiet with the environmental and other costs of rapid and largely unregulated industrial growth, together with its attendant urban sprawl, had produced vocal mass organisations demanding remedial action. In 1971 the international economic system that had contributed so much to Japanese economic development began to unravel. And then in 1973 Japan was hit by the 'oil shock'.

The Era of Political Stability

Ikeda Hayato, who replaced the discredited Kishi Nobusuke as prime minister in July 1960, was a former ministry of finance bureaucrat enticed into politics by Yoshida Shigeru during the occupation. Ikeda sought to project a personality and a political style which contrasted sharply with that of his predecessor, whose arrogance and confrontational postures had done much to polarise Japanese politics and public life. The new prime minister 'cultivated a soothing image. . . . He undertook a studied humility in foreign as well as domestic affairs' (Havens, 1967: 19). Ikeda very quickly stamped a conciliatory character on his new administration. The government intervened to settle the Miike mining dispute which had gone on for more than 300 days. Ikeda's style was characterised by 'low posture' politics which avoided controversial and divisive issues. He played down relations with the United States to avoid stirring those violent emotions which had burst to the surface in 1960, and he kept well clear of the thorny issue of constitutional revision. Instead, he concentrated on the economy and, in particular, would become personally linked with the Income Doubling Plan. Ikeda had a deep interest in and great knowledge of economic issues. He had been an economic bureaucrat before entering politics and during his political career he had been a minister in both the Ministry of Finance and MITI. Ikeda understood that economic growth was the issue which caused least division amongst the Japanese. By concentrating on the economy, he sought to rebuild a national consensus out of the tumult of the Kishi period.

Ikeda could claim success in his economic policies and

objectives and he was a popular prime minister. On the other hand, Ikeda's stewardship of the LDP was unsatisfactory. During his premiership, factional strife within the party intensified. Initially, Ikeda had been supported by the important factions led by Satō and Kishi, but these influential figures in the party came to fear that Ikeda was becoming too powerful; Satō in particular was afraid that he would never become prime minister if Ikeda was allowed to plant his influence too deeply within the LDP. When Ikeda in 1964 sought a third term as LDP president, and therefore another two years as prime minister, his allies defected and Satō Eisaku, Kishi's protégé, challenged Ikeda. The LDP presidential elections of July 1964 produced unprecedented levels of bribery and corruption, wrapping conservative politics in a fog of disrepute. Ikeda used his business contacts to marshal vast quantities of money to buy support in the party and he was able beat Satō by four votes – but his triumph was shortlived. He was diagnosed as suffering from terminal cancer and forced to resign as prime minister in November 1964 (Scalapino, 1962).

The LDP faction leaders decided to avoid the expense, and odium, of another unseemly election for the party presidency, by agreeing to support Satō Eisaku; confusingly, Satō was Kishi Nobusuke's natural brother but he had been adopted by another family. Satō was another former bureaucrat who Yoshida had attracted into politics from the upper reaches of the Ministry of Transport. He was a lacklustre, uncharismatic figure but this did not prevent him from becoming the longest-serving premier in Japanese history. What he lacked in charisma, Satō compensated for through his ability to manipulate the rival factions through extremely skilful appointments. He was so adept at this that he became popularly known as 'Satō the personnel manager' (Curtis, 1988: 99). In 1964–5 Satō's canny domination of the LDP was buttressed when death removed his three greatest rivals within the party. Their personal factions fragmented and many gravitated into Satō's own faction. During his tenure of office Satō might have expected a challenge from the two rising stars of the LDP, Fukuda Takeo, leader of the Kishi faction, and Tanaka Kakuei, who oversaw the day-to-day management of his own faction. Satō blunted possible challenges to his leadership from either man by cleverly exploiting the intense rivalry, and personal hatred, between Fukuda and Tanaka.

The Emergence of a Multi-Party System

The LDP owed its monopoly of office between 1955 and 1993 as much to the weaknesses of the opposition parties that emerged in the 1960s as to its own efforts and strengths. The evolution of this conservative domination was accelerated by the transformation of Japan's political structure from a two-party to a multi-party system, as the number of opposition political parties increased and the anti-LDP popular vote splintered. In the first House of Representatives election after the unification of both the conservative and socialist parties in 1958, the LDP and JSP won 99.5 per cent of the seats taken by party candidates. By the 1972 House of Representatives election, the two main parties' share of the seats had fallen to 81.5 per cent. The chief victim in this haemorrhage of electoral support from the two largest parties was the JSP. In 1958 the party had received 32.9 per cent of the popular vote, but by 1972 this had fallen to 21.9 per cent. The multi-member constituency electoral system distorted the effect of this fall in the popular vote on parliamentary representation. In 1958 the JSP had won 166 seats, by 1972 this had fallen to 118 – though this was a significant improvement on the disastrous 1969 election in which socialist representation had fallen to ninety seats.

The steep decline in the electoral fortunes of the JSP was the result of a number of developments. The right-wing defections in 1959–60, which had led to the foundation of the rival Democratic Socialist Party (DSP) in 1960, altered the left–right balance of the JSP in favour of the radicals. In the early 1960s the JSP leader, Eda Saburō, had tried to reorient the party's platform towards a more gradualist, non-revolutionary socialism. Eda's grip on the party was loosened by the loss of part of the right wing of the JSP in 1959, and by 1965 he had been ousted. The fevered domestic and international atmosphere of the second half of the 1960s contributed to the JSP's lurch in the direction of extremism (Stockwin, 1986).

In addition to its internal difficulties, the JSP was damaged by a revival in the fortunes of its old enemy, the JCP, and by the appearance of new political parties which ate into the JSP's popular support. Between 1960 and 1972 the breakaway DSP collected between 6.9 and 8.7 per cent of the popular vote and obtained between nineteen and thirty-one seats in House of Representatives, largely at the expense of the JSP. The founding of Kōmeitō (Clean Government Party) in 1964 hit the JSP severely. By 1972 Kōmeitō was getting over 8 per cent of the popular vote, which translated into twenty-nine seats in the lower house; surveys showed that around one-third of Kōmeitō voters had previously been supporters of the JSP. Both the reviving JCP and the new Kōmeitō projected positive images with their committed, focused and active organisations and rapidly growing memberships, whilst the JSP, almost totally reliant on the Sōhyō trade union federation for both money and membership, seemed to be an anachronism. High-speed growth had grim social and political implications for the JSP. Growing prosperity and changing social perceptions naturally altered political choices. The JSP, dominated by the radical Sōhyō establishment, was unable adequately to respond to these extensive socio-economic changes. Sōhyō would not permit the party to move from a 'class-based' party to a 'mass' party since it would weaken Sōhyō's grip on the JSP. Since the number of Japanese who identified themselves as members of that class whose interests the JSP claimed to champion was shrinking rapidly, the failure of the party of broaden its appeal was electorally disastrous. The political impact of these social changes was reflected in structural change in the base of support for the JSP. During the 1960s the JSP steadily lost support in its old heartlands of the Kantō and Kansai industrial belts. By 1972 the party was doing better in rural and small town constituencies than in the cities and larger towns (Hrebenar, 1986).

The Democratic Socialist Party did not develop as a viable alternative to either the LDP or the JSP. When Nishio Suehiro led the defection from the JSP, the newly founded DSP had forty members in the House of Representatives. In the general election held in November 1960 this was slashed to seventeen seats and the DSP has never subsequently reached its original parliamentary strength, approaching it only in the 1983 general election when it had thirty-eight candidates elected to the House of Representatives. The DSP became increasingly identified as the political wing of Dōmei, a trade union federation that materialised from moderate unions which had broken away from the militant Sōhyō union movement in the early 1960s. The DSP also attracted support from some of the new syncretic religious movements which were becoming popular in the 1960s and 1970s. None the less, the DSP remained a small party, geographically concentrated in the greater Tokyo region, Kyoto–Osaka–Kobe and in and around Nagoya. These were precisely the areas where support for the JSP was ebbing away in the 1960s and the 6–8 per cent of the popular vote that the DSP could usually command represented a further blow to JSP electoral prospects (Hrebenar et al., 1986).

The revival of the Japan Communist Party contributed to the erosion of the JSP. Founded in July 1922, the JCP was Japan's oldest political party. Before the end of the Second World War, the party's main experience was repression as its leading lights were imprisoned. The occupation temporarily brought the JCP into mainstream politics, and a new leader, Nosaka Sanzō, tried to make the regenerated communist party 'loveable'. The loveable party would play down revolutionary activity and declare its devotion to achieving its ends solely by parliamentary means. After moderate showings in the 1946 and 1947 general elections, the JCP did extremely well in the 1949 general election, receiving almost 10 per cent of the popular vote and getting thirty-five seats in the House of Representatives. This progress was abruptly halted by a radical change of direction forced upon the JCP by Moscow. In January 1950 Cominform, the postwar successor to the Communist International, denounced the 'loveable' policies of Nosaka and urged a much more militant approach. The outbreak of the Korean War led the JCP to swerve further to the left. The government, with SCAP support, seized the opportunity offered by increased communist militancy to try to crush the party. Using the occupation's purging power the Yoshida government excluded members of the party's central committee from public office. Some communist leaders went underground whilst others fled to Peking; rank and file members made abortive attempts to sponsor terrorism and sabotage. This alienated substantial segments of the electorate and, coupled with the effects of the purge and flight of the party's leadership, led to the JCP's representation in the House of Representatives being wiped out in the general election of October 1952.

For the next fifteen years the JCP remained in the electoral wilderness. Until 1969 the party never had more than five members in the House of Representatives and at best polled only 4.7 per cent of the popular vote. Within the party, however, significant developments were taking place. In 1955 Miyamoto Kenji became effective leader of the JCP and he was to be the most important single figure in the party for over thirty years. Under Miyamoto's skilful guidance the JCP progressively severed its close ties with the international communist movement and moved in the same direction as the Eurocommunists, seeking to follow a road to socialism through a parliamentary, rather than a revolutionary, strategy. These new moves to 'loveability' steadily restored the JCP's electoral appeal. In 1969 the party polled 6.8 per cent of the vote and in 1972 the party was able to exceed its 1949 high point, obtaining 10.4 per cent of the popular vote. The net effect of this revival of the JCP, however, was to splinter the non-LDP vote still further. The electoral system used to elect the House of Representatives magnified the effect disproportionately, to the benefit of the LDP (Berton, 1986).

The foundation of an entirely new party, Kōmeitō, usually translated as the Clean Government Party, on 17 November 1964, was not only another stage in the emergence of a multi-party political system but also an unprecedented event in Japanese history. Kōmeitō was unique because it was the only Japanese political party to be based on religion, representing the political wing of Sōka Gakkai, an evangelical Buddhist organisation. Sōka Gakkai had flirted with politics since 1954 when it had fielded candidates in local elections; in 1956 two Sōka Gakkai-sponsored candidates were elected to the House of Representatives. Members of the movement continued to gain electoral support, and Kōmeitō was established as a formal political party in November 1964 to put some distance between the religious and political activities of Sōka Gakkai, as well as to provide the organisational means to focus its political activities (Hayes, 1992).

Sōka Gakkai almost certainly did not have the 16 million members it claimed in 1960 but the sect's undoubtedly large membership constituted a promising reservoir of support which the new party very quickly tapped. On the other hand, Kōmeitō's close connection with Sōka Gakkai was also an electoral liability since many Japanese harboured dark suspicions about the organisation. Kōmeitō's position in the political spectrum was slightly left of centre, although it is difficult to classify the party's political complexion precisely since its platform of policies was nebulous, proclaiming as it did general support for world peace, humanitarian socialism, Buddhist democracy and an end to corruption in politics. In the first lower house elections that the Kōmeitō contested in January 1967, the party received 5.3 per cent of the vote and took twenty-five seats; by the 1969 election Kōmeitō strength had stabilised at around 10 per cent of the popular vote. Initially Kōmeitō probably took more voters from the LDP than from the JSP, but the party's parent movement, Sōka Gakkai, was most active and successful in recruiting members to the religion in the large conurbations, precisely those areas where the socialist vote was eroding. Again, this latest split in the opposition vote benefited the ruling LDP because the effects of the splintering of the opposition vote was magnified by the multi-member, one-person/one-vote system used to elect the House of Representatives.

During the 1960s the foundations of LDP dominance in Japanese politics solidified. The LDP became firmly identified as the party of economic success. The active sponsorship of rapid economic growth, symbolised by the Income Doubling Plan peddled by Ikeda, channelled the LDP into an area of public policy in which there was a widespread popular consensus, certainly compared to fissiparous issues such as constitutional revision and relations with the United States. The image of the LDP as a bastion of stability dates from the Ikeda era. Even though faction leaders rebelled against such stability to push their own leadership claims, the longevity of the Ikeda, and particularly of the Satō, administrations reinforced this aura of stability. The LDP proved extremely skilful at adjusting to the social changes brought by rapid industrialisation and urbanisation. The party constantly adjusted its appeal to attract the urbanised middle classes who were a social result of high-speed growth. Equally, the party was careful to maintain its appeal to its traditional supporters in the countryside by maintaining policies favouring agriculture. The splintering of the opposition and the development of a multi-party system, bringing with it the erosion of the main opposition party, the JSP, favoured the LDP. This advantage was enhanced by the singular system used for elections to the House of Representatives. Negatively, the more unseemly aspects of the LDP worsened in the 1960s and would plague the party for three decades. During the Ikeda and Satō years, personalised factions became entrenched in the LDP, and a miasma of corruption and illegality enveloped them. The grand scandals surfaced after 1973, but the seeds for them were sown in the LDP structure which crystallised in the 1960s.

The second half of the era of political stability was distinguished by the emergence of popular protest movements. Mass political activity had trailed off after the 1960 Security Treaty crisis. From the mid-1960s, however, popular movements emerged from a number of different causes. The immediate catalyst was the Vietnam War. In 1965 the League for Peace in Vietnam (*Beheiren*) was established, awakening a number of other hitherto relatively dormant groups. Protest against the Vietnam War coalesced with the left-leaning anti-nuclear movement, and also became caught up with student protest orchestrated by *Zengakuren*, the nationwide radical student movement. Initially, these movements attracted considerable support, until serious disruption in many of Japan's most prestigious universities in 1968 and the failure of a campaign to prevent the renewal of the Security Treaty in 1970 led to these radical protest groups melting away.

More significant was the mass movement which appeared from 1967 in protest against almost uncontrolled pollution. The anti-pollution movement reached down to grass-roots level and was provoked by the enormous environmental and other costs of high-speed growth. Although the anti-pollution and environmental protest movements were never organised or structured, they represented a level of popular disquiet and disillusion that neither the government nor business interests could ignore. The LDP government's responses to the anti-pollution movement varied from the imposition of the world's most stringent restrictions on vehicle exhaust gases to Tanaka Kakuei's grand strategy of remodelling the Japanese archipelago (White, 1993). The anti-pollution movement had some impact upon environmental politics in Japan and it did prompt the LDP to reconsider and reorientate some of its policies, but it did not have lasting political significance. The most bizarre act of protest was committed by Mishima Yukio, postwar Japan's most distinguished novelist. Mishima, a celebrated pillar of the extreme right, attempted a *coup d'état* to restore what he identified as the forces of traditional Japan. When he and a small group of followers attempted to take over a Self Defence Force barracks in central Tokyo on 25 November 1970, they met with a barrage of derision. Mishima and some of his acolytes responded by committing ritual suicide, an event that horrified the Japanese but had no measurable effect on support of the extreme right.

The Dimensions of High-Speed Growth

The period from the late 1950s to 1973 was the zenith of postwar Japan's economic growth. In the late 1950s and early 1960s these factors that would produce high-speed growth were put in place. The dimensions of that economic growth were breathtaking. Between 1960 and 1969 the growth in Japan's GNP averaged 12.1 per cent per year, more than twice the growth rate of the next most successful developed economy. Japan's growth rate eased off between 1970 and the first oil shock in 1973, averaging 7.5 per cent per annum, but it was still the world's highest. Growth in certain individual sectors was even more impressive. In the decade from 1961 to 1971, manufacturing grew at 14 per cent per annum, whilst machinery manufacturing expanded by 19.6 per cent per annum. In 1959 Japan's national income was calculated as being ¥14,912 billion, by 1971 it had more than tripled to ¥46,907 billion. Between 1960 and 1973, labour productivity increased on average 10.7 per cent per year in Japan, reflecting high levels of investment in new technology as well as the generally high and improving quality of the workforce. In the same period, West Germany achieved barely half of the Japanese rate of growth in productivity, with 5.5 per cent per annum, whilst the United Kingdom was limited to 4.3 per cent and the United States to a mere 3 per cent. Between 1965 and 1970 the growth in labour productivity in Japan averaged a staggering 13.4 per cent per year. By 1965 Japan had become the world's second largest economy.

The scale of Japan's economic success was first revealed to the outside world by the *Economist* in September 1962. Since then, the sources and secrets of Japanese growth have been sought as a form of contemporary economist's philosopher's stone. This quest has profound economic and political overtones and has resulted in a vast range of explanations for Japan's dynamic economic expansion being offered. At one end of the spectrum of analysis of this economic 'miracle' was the neo-classical economic view that 'Japanese growth was not miraculous: it can be reasonably well understood and explained by ordinary economic causes' (Nakamura, 1987: 6). Diametrically opposed explanations sought to isolate institutions and qualities vital to rapid economic growth that were unique to Japanese culture, society, values or historical experience (Morishima, 1982). The reality is that 'neither a purely economic model nor a purely cultural model is adequate for analysis of the post-war . . . economy' (Lincoln, 1988: 33).

'Japan Incorporated' and Japanese Economic Growth

The favourite popular explanation of Japanese economic growth centred on the concept of 'Japan Incorporated'. Indeed, the notion of 'Japan Inc.' may be unique amongst scholarly theses in becoming the subject of a best-selling comic book. 'Japan Inc.' represents a sophisticated argument about the role of government and bureaucracy in the 'miracle'. It identifies a close, almost symbiotic, relationship between Japan's conservative politicians, who dominated government from the end of the occupation, the country's prestigious and powerful bureaucracy, and the leadership of big business. A number of factors serve to bind these three groups together. For instance, most members of all three groups are composed of graduates of Japan's élite universities, especially Tokyo University, and they share a commitment to rapid economic growth. The most important bond is provided by bureaucrats and those ex-bureaucrats who retire and perform *amakudari*, 'descent from heaven', which leads them both into the LDP and into the higher management of the large companies and organisations that represent big business, especially the Federation of Economic Organizations, *Keidanren*. These ex-bureaucrats in politics and big business retain contacts with their former colleagues in the civil service and provide channels through which bureaucratic influence in government and the largest of Japan's companies and economic institutions is extended.

Observers who emphasise the role of 'Japan Inc.' see its three components operating in unison to accomplish the aim of rapid economic growth. The chosen instrument to achieve high-speed growth was 'industrial policy'. This was framed essentially by the economic bureaucracy and involved the administration and the state deciding on the allocation of investment capital, raw materials and labour rather than on this being left to market forces (Komiya *et al.*, 1988). This industrial policy was then delivered to business and industry for implementation through 'administrative guidance', informal instructions from the powerful economic ministries to private corporations and companies. Naturally, the industrial policy was part of a co-ordinated strategy for economic, especially industrial, growth. Within the orbit of 'Japan Inc.' potential disputes between government, bureaucracy and big business could be amicably defused, so that the push to high-speed growth emerges as consensus. In its purest form, 'Japan Inc.' has been seen as a high-level conspiracy by the Japanese political, bureaucratic and business élites to establish Japan's worldwide economic dominance. According to the conspiracy theorists, the normal functioning of the market economy and competition is stifled and, if necessary, democratic and parliamentary processes are subverted to achieve the ultimate goal of dominance of the world economy by Japan. Most scholars of the 'Japan Inc.' school are more considered and restrained. They argue that there is a close collaborative relationship between government, bureaucracy and big business which plans and co-ordinates grand strategy for Japan's economic development and which greatly enhances the ability of the economic bureaucracy to shape Japan's economic future. A more subtle rendering of this analysis contends that Japan has developed particularly effective bureaucratic instruments to guide the economy, especially in the guise of MITI, so that the close relationships at the pinnacles of government and politics, the civil service and big business ensure that private companies obey the 'administrative guidance' given by MITI.

Rival analysts of postwar Japan's rapid economic growth argue that the 'industrial policy' of the government and the burcaucracy has, at best, only a marginal role in inducing and guiding the 'miracle', and at worst may actually have obstructed it. There is no easy or complete explanation of the contribution of the state to the 'miracle' (Eades and Yamamura, 1987). The government and bureaucracy did inherit a powerful battery of instruments which could be used to control the economy. None the less, even in the 1950s, when the bureaucracy's power over the economy was at its greatest and when they were most anxious to dampen 'excessive' competition, there were occasions when private companies were willing to defy 'administrative guidance'. The best known instance was in 1956–7 when Toyota challenged the Isuzu Company's monopoly in diesel-powered trucks. MITI believed that Japan did not need two truck manufacturers and 'advised' Toyota to drop its diesel truck manufacture. The chairman of Toyota responded that 'the government has no right to tell us to stop. Toyota will continue selling diesel trucks even if the ministry is against it', and MITI's 'administrative guidance' was ignored. Generally, the degree of influence and control that the state has been able to exercise over the private sector has decreased with time. Despite the well-documented case of truck production, the Ministry of Finance, MITI and other ministries were able to wield considerable power because they largely controlled foreign exchange, raw material allocation and access to investment capital. As the economy grew and government levers on it diminished, so the power of the state receded.

In some spheres the contribution of the state to postwar economic success is clear and non-controversial. The maintenance and improvement of the national education system provided Japan with a first-rate workforce which was a key to industrial growth. The conservative monopoly of government both created a political environment conducive to growth and provided great political stability; this eased the problems of decision making for private corporations and companies. The contentious issue is the extent to which the state has been a direct instrument, a shaper of economic growth. Unfortunately, the contribution of the government and the bureaucracy and of their 'industrial policy' and 'administrative guidance' to the creation of the postwar world's most successful economy ultimately defies measurement. The very close connections that have developed between the conservative political élite, the bureaucracy and the leaders of Japan's vanguard companies since the late 1940s created vital consensus between the pinnacles of government, administration and management. This consensus was a vital ingredient of industrial development in postwar Japan (Okimoto, 1989). To what extent the state, either politicians or bureaucrats, was the dominant voice in this economic decision-making triad sadly remains unclear.

Investment, Technology and High-Speed Growth

The single most important source of economic growth between 1953 and 1971 was massive inputs of capital investment (Denison and Chung, 1976). Heavy investment, largely by private industry, equipped Japanese industry with the best technology that could be bought, maintaining the best of Japan's industries at the cutting edge of technology. This also allowed the necessary productive resources to meet domestic and international demand, which burgeoned in

110

the late 1950s and particularly in the 1960s. Most of the investment capital that large-scale industry used came from the major banks. These were able to supply unusually large sums of investment capital for two reasons. Government guarantees allowed the banks to continue the policy of 'overloan', lending more money than financial orthodoxy would indicate. In addition, Japan historically had a very high rate of personal savings, providing the commercial banks with huge deposits which they processed into investment capital for industry. Furthermore, in the postwar period the nature of some of the conglomerates changed. Banks became the central institutions of these reorganised conglomerates and provided ample, often cheap, investment capital to other members of the group.

Much of this investment capital went into buying new technology from abroad. Japan's prewar economic growth, especially its industrial development, had been fundamentally dependent on the import of foreign technology (Minami, 1986). Importing the latest technology was a vital factor in the era of high-speed growth. The technological base of Japan's industry had advanced significantly immediately before, and during, the Second World War. Nevertheless, the technological gap between Japan and the west, and especially with the United States, had widened rather than narrowed during the war. Until the early 1950s hardly any new technology was imported into Japan to correct this imbalance. Then, under the strict supervision of the government, the inflow surged. Between 1951 and 1955 payments for the import of foreign technology grew on average 31.5 per cent each year, accelerating to 34 per cent between 1955 and 1961. Between 1964 and 1971 Japan paid more for foreign knowhow than any other major industrial country (Peck and Tamura, 1976). In the 1950s imports of technology, largely from the United States, modernised basic industries, such as iron, steel and electricity. Then, imported electrically-powered machinery was used in developing industries, such as automobiles, and specific technologies trickled down into other industries. In the period of high-speed growth foreign technology was imported in great quantities and was at the core of that growth. Extremely high rates of investment ensured that the most modern technology was available and used in the advanced sectors of Japan's economy. Between 1953 and 1971 technology was the most important single input into rapid economic growth. In the decade after 1960 it has been calculated that technology was responsible for 45 per cent of Japan's growth rate (Ito, 1992).

By 1967 Japan was rapidly developing its own research and development capabilities. The rate of growth in expenditure on research accelerated rapidly in the second half of the 1960s as large Japanese companies, especially electrical manufacturers, became technologically self-sufficient. Japan's advances in research and development were especially important to the overall growth of the economy because, unlike the United States or Britain, they were almost entirely unrelated to military research, and hence were directly useful to the civilian industrial economy. Closing the technology gap had a negative side. It was the most important single reason for slowing down Japan's rate of economic growth in the early 1970s, even before the first oil shock. The easy growth of the 1950s and 1960s had come in part from simply importing and using western technology to increase production. Japan had benefited from being a relative latecomer, able to buy in and equip its factories with the latest technology from the west. In future, Japanese industry had to generate technological advance through its own research and development, and this moderated the rate of industrial growth (Lincoln, 1988).

The Japanese People and the Economic 'Miracle'

Even in the mid-1950s Japan was still a predominantly rural society. The American-imposed land reforms had created a rural society of peasant landowners and, even in 1955, half of Japan's working population was still engaged in agriculture. After the reforms, agricultural production increased. In the 1950s and 1960s increased agricultural production was particularly marked. This occurred for reasons that ultimately caused problems both for Japanese agriculture and, more generally, for Japan's economic relations with the outside world. In the 1950s and 1960s Japanese farming went through a process of rapid mechanisation. Small powered hand-tillers spread quickly: in 1955 there were 89,000 of these machines in Japan but by 1970 the figure had reached 3.45 million. This 'mini-tractorisation' made it possible for younger farmers to take employment in nearby factories, becoming essentially part-time farmers. The technological developments in small-scale agricultural machinery made it possible for much of the work on small farms to be handled by retired farmers and their wives. These small-scale farms, supplemented by industrial employment, meant that farming became economically viable. Thus, Japanese government attempts begun in 1961 to increase the size of farms and hence make them more economic failed. By 1984 85 per cent of farming was part-time (Hayami, 1988). The survival of small-scale farming made it politically and socially necessary for the government to continue to subsidise agriculture, creating a series of niggling and increasingly serious trade disputes with the United States as the government maintained import bans and restrictions to protect agriculture.

It was the changing structure of the Japanese workforce in the decade after Japan was restored to independence which transformed it from a rural and agricultural society to one which was overwhelmingly urban and employed in manufacturing and service industries. In the 1950s that half of the working population who were engaged in agriculture and other primary production became a large reservoir of labour which flowed into the urban factories as rapid industrial growth got under way. The speed of this transfer of labour was astonishing. In 1950 50 per cent of young people leaving middle and high schools went into agriculture; by

1960 this had dropped to 10 per cent and by 1965 it was only 5 per cent.

The Japanese workforce was a decisive component of the surge that the economy experienced in the 1960s and early 1970s. The two aspects to this key contribution were the high quality of the workforce itself and the institutions and methods that emerged to manage that labour force. The mass of the population in 1950 had basic education, but the levels of education were increasing. In 1955, only 38 per cent of those entering the workforce had been educated beyond middle-school level, but this proportion had increased to 58 per cent by 1965 and a decade later the figure was 91 per cent. These high, and very rapidly rising, levels of education were to be a key component in creating a high-quality labour force able to take advantage of rising levels of investment in high-technology production facilities and methods (Rohlen, 1992).

Management techniques developed to exploit this high-quality labour force played an important part in fostering high levels of productivity and flexibility. Lifetime employment, seniority wages and enterprise unions – the so-called 'three sacred treasures' which operated in the large companies – contributed to productivity and company loyalty. However, the effectiveness of these management methods in securing industrial harmony should not be overstated. Industrial relations in Japan during the two decades of highest growth, between 1955 and 1973, were not spectacularly good. In these years, Japan had far more strikes per 1,000 workers than West Germany and Sweden, falling only a little below the levels of industrial strife experienced in the United Kingdom and France in the 1960s. The worst time was in 1959 and 1960 when there were several high-profile, serious industrial disputes, first in the steel industry and then at the Miike coal mine belonging to the Mitsui Coal Company. The Miike dispute was especially bitter, lasting nearly a year, and it was only settled by the direct intervention of the Ikeda government. However, just as the polarised, violent politics of 1960 were replaced by a gentler, more consensual style of government under Ikeda, so the violent industrial disputes of 1959–60 led to substantial improvements in industrial relations. More moderate leadership gained control of some of the key trade unions and they recoiled from the confrontation of the previous decade. On the other side, Japanese management came to accept 'the philosophy of co-operative and conciliatory labor relations' (Aoki, 1987).

By the mid-1960s the Japanese management style and the structures within which this style could prosper were substantially in place in the large-scale companies at the forefront of Japan's high-speed growth. There was no totally uniform Japanese management style, yet managers tended to have certain distinctive characteristics which contributed to Japan's economic success. Japanese management placed less emphasis on maximising profit than their counterparts in Europe and North America. Conversely, they tended to have a greater concern for employees' interests when framing and implementing their corporate policies. The 'three sacred treasures', plus a strong strain of paternalism, led the large companies to provide a whole range of welfare benefits for both employees and their immediate families. The three 'treasures' had appeared first in larger Japanese enterprises in the second decade of the twentieth century. Along with another characteristic of modern industrial relations, the twice-yearly bonus, which also made its appearance around the time of the First World War, lifetime employment and seniority wages were part of a strategy to retain scarce skilled workers (Suzuki, 1991). Enterprise labour unions, in which all employees of a company belong to that company's union, irrespective of trade or function, were a creation of the first postwar decade (Nakamura, 1981).

This management style was helped by the environment in which professional managers operated. Management was substantially free of serious control by owners of companies, boards of directors, or shareholders. Historically, many of the elements of this style and structure of management developed out of practices in place before the Pacific War. This 'Japanese Enterprise System' was greatly assisted by a number of developments that took place between 1945 and 1965. In 1946 and 1947 the occupation authorities broke the grip that the old owning families and their holding companies had over the *zaibatsu*. SCAP did not break up the *zaibatsu* as they had originally intended, but the families and holding companies lost control permanently. Shares were sold off by the occupation authorities, although no one was allowed to hold more than 1 per cent of a company. Ownership, which had been the basis of control in the prewar conglomerates, was widely scattered, and the power of ownership was heavily diluted. Further, the economic purges removed the top layer of *zaibatsu* management, creating space for younger, and usually more flexible, managers, creating a 'managerial revolution from above' (Aoki, 1987: 268–9). During the late 1940s and early 1950s the rights and influence that the trade unions had gained during the first phase of the occupation were clawed back by government and management, leaving the road open for the emergence of the enterprise union system. To compensate for the weakening of the unions, management in the large companies improved the conditions of employees by building upon practices which had emerged in the 1920s and 1930s, such as lifetime employment and seniority wages.

Postwar Japan's industrial structure has to a considerable extent retained the distinctive dualist pattern which characterised the prewar economy. The dominant force in the economy were the *keiretsu* (or, to use a derogatory term, *zaikai*), a small number of very large conglomerates, often connecting a variety of different sectors through close linkages between banks, financial institutions, manufacturing companies and trading companies. Much of what the outside world has perceived as the Japanese enterprise system is in fact the normal operating and management customs of the *keiretsu*. The other part of the economy consists of a huge number of medium and especially small-scale firms. Many of the small-scale enterprises are either family-owned subcontracting firms or, more commonly, family-run shops. Such a dualist economic structure is by no means unusual

116

in itself. In the 1950s the proportion of workers in Japan employed in firms with less than fifty employees was only a little higher than in Italy and West Germany, although very high compared to the United States or Britain. However, the wage and productivity differentials between the various parts of the dualist economy in Japan were unusually high. In the United States the value added per worker in small-scale manufacturing firms was 70 per cent of the largest firms, whilst in Japan the figure was only 25 per cent. This dual economic structure was not, of course, a product of the postwar period. The *keiretsu* were the natural, if not always the lineal, successors to the prewar *zaibatsu*, although in terms of ownership, management, number and structure they differed appreciably from their prewar cousins, whilst since the 1920s Japan's prewar economy had exhibited particularly high levels of industrial dualism.

The domestic market was the basic engine of high-speed growth, yet Japan's rapid economic growth in the 1950s and 1960s was heavily dependent upon the prevailing international economic climate. The international monetary stability provided by the Bretton Woods system, and the liberal trading regime resulting from GATT were vital components in Japan's economic growth. In 1965 Japan's balance of payments entered a long phase of surplus, thereby removing the balance of payments ceiling on growth. Ironically, just as international restraint on the domestic Japanese economy disappeared, the beneficial economic environment came under threat. Stability in the Bretton Woods system was based on a fixed rate of convertibility between the US dollar and gold. The strains of the Vietnam War, and other economic problems in the United States, forced the administration of President Richard Nixon to suspend the convertibility of the dollar into gold on 15 August 1971. At a stroke the relative international monetary stability of the previous twenty-five years evaporated. Japan had pegged the yen at $1 = ¥360 in 1949 and this rate was maintained until 1971. The yen had become increasingly undervalued and this had benefited Japanese exports enormously. The

Japanese government was anxious to maintain the old parity, but pressure to revalue was intense. Japan's international competitors regarded this attempt to keep the yen undervalued as sharp practice. In December 1971, as part of the international Smithsonian Agreement, the Japanese agreed to a new exchange rate of $1 = ¥308. This did not survive and the yen continued to appreciate. The Satō government tried to cushion the economy by pumping money into it, but this simply stimulated inflation just before the blow of the oil shock in November 1973 (Uchino, 1983).

The first 'oil shock' in 1973 brought the golden age of Japan's economy symbolically to an end. In reality, high-speed growth had been slowing before the shock, but 1973 did represent a trauma for the Japanese. It highlighted what was seen as the fragility of the economic 'miracle'. Economic growth would seem much more difficult after 1973. Nevertheless, between 1960 and 1973 the Japanese economy had grown at an unprecedented rate. Furthermore, Japan's political structure appeared much more stable than before 1960. Ikeda and Satō had provided a comforting sense of stability to many Japanese and the permanent monopoly of government by the conservatives seemed guaranteed by the splintering of the opposition. During the heady period of high-speed growth the standard of living in Japan had risen enormously; between 1955 and 1973 the rate of growth in consumption was statistically almost identical to the rate of economic growth (Horioka, 1993). None the less there was a perception that public amenities had been sacrificed on the altar of economic development, resulting in enormous environmental damage which was only beginning to be remedied by 1973. The following two decades were notable for growing demands for the fruits of the economic miracle to be reflected in the quality of life.

5

The Miracle Falters: The Oil Shocks, the Economy and Politics

On 6 July 1972 Japan's prime minister, Satō Eisaku, stepped down in favour of his faction manager, Tanaka Kakuei. Satō had been the longest-serving prime minister in Japanese history, having held office since 1964, and he symbolised a period of unprecedented political stability for Japan. Between 1960 and 1972 only two men had held the office of prime minister but in the next ten years there would be five incumbents of the office. In fact, between the departure of Satō and 1994 only one of Japan's thirteen prime ministers, Nakasone Yasuhiro, would survive more than two years in office. Paradoxically, this bewildering turnover at the top of government did not seriously loosen the LDP's grip on power. The party found itself swimming in difficult political waters but showed itself equal to the challenge of a new phase in Japanese politics. The LDP steadily built new bases of support throughout the 1970s, in part by meeting the demands from the new, urban, industrial working and middle classes for more social amenities and greater social welfare, and in part by extending industrial development beyond the great conurbations along the Pacific coast to other parts of Japan. To curry favour with the new social groupings that had been forged by rapid industrialisation and urbanisation the LDP also refocused government spending, switching resources from agriculture to welfare and amenities (Curtis, 1988). The 1970 budget had allocated 11.3 per cent of spending to agriculture whilst the whole area of health and welfare got only 13.7 per cent. By 1975 the proportions were reversed with 19 per cent devoted to health and welfare whilst agriculture received only 10.2 per cent of spending. By 1983, agriculture accounted for only 6.1 per cent of government expenditure, compared to 18.3 per cent going on health and welfare. The LDP was using state revenue to redefine the sources of its electoral support; it was moving from a rural to an urban base in response to changing social conditions. This strategy worked. The LDP went into the 1970s as a party whose grip on government was under threat; by the end of the decade, despite a number of scandals, it was apparently the permanent party of government. The political achievement of the LDP was all the more remarkable because it took place against a background of serious economic problems caused by the oil shocks that shook the world economy in the 1970s.

The Politics of Instability

Instability in the LDP leadership was one result of a changing party and political climate. By the early 1970s, the LDP's grip on government seemed anything but permanent. The party's popular vote, and the number of seats it obtained in the House of Representatives, declined in the general elections of 1972 and 1976. In part this was the result of growing popular dissatisfaction at the costs and consequences of high-speed growth and dissatisfaction at the unwillingness, or inability, of the government adequately to address the problems. Changing demographic and social patterns in Japan threatened a new and trying political environment for the LDP. The LDP was gaining support in urban Japan but voters in the countryside remained extremely important to it. Thus, the relative demographic decline of rural Japan, the LDP's traditional base of support, was very ominous for the party. The immediate problems of the LDP in the 1970s were also the result of Tanaka Kakuei's entanglement in a series of scandals, most particularly in the Lockheed affair. As the party became increasingly enmeshed in the scandal, it threatened to split apart: in 1974 a number of reform-minded LDP parliamentarians broke away to form a new party, the New Liberal Club.

Tanaka Kakuei was one of the most important figures to appear on postwar Japan's political stage; he also became one of the most vilified. He did not come from the normal mould for LDP politicians. Tanaka was very much a self-made man, without a university education, who before entering politics had made a fortune from construction in his native Niigata, a deprived area on the Japan Sea coast. Throughout his public career, he retained both his heavy regional accent and his rough and ready mode of expression. Tanaka came to be regarded as representing all that was wrong with the corrupt, 'money politics' within the LDP yet, in 1972, when he became prime minister, his appointment was widely welcomed in the party. Tanaka had been Satō's faction manager and had become extremely skilled at manipulating the members of this faction into what one Japanese commentator called 'organisational clientelism'.

Since 1966 Tanaka had increasingly clashed with the powerful Fukuda Takeo, a faction leader who, as an ex-bureaucrat, was widely regarded as the natural successor to Satō. To counter Fukuda's ambitions, Tanaka used his intimate knowledge of the Satō faction to build up his own personal following within it. He was particularly successful in attracting younger parliamentarians, upon whom Tanaka showered money. In the 1972 contest for the LDP presidency, and therefore the premiership, Fukuda and Tanaka together are said to have distributed ¥5 billion, an average of ¥10 million for each of the 487 LDP parliamentarians who had a vote. Tanaka's skill in distributing money, and in manipulating the faction system, exceeded that of Fukuda. He defeated the heir-apparent, won the party presidency and succeeded to the premiership (Nester, 1990; Tomita *et al.*, 1986).

When Tanaka came to office in July 1972, the LDP's grip on government was shaky. He set about trying to stem the tide of criticism which had developed from the mass movements protesting against pollution, and demanding action to adjust geographical imbalances in development and to improve social welfare and amenities. Tanaka astutely developed the so-called Japan Archipelago plan and became a devotee of anti-pollution and social welfare legislation. To pay for these policies Tanaka attempted a financial conjuring trick. The 1973 budget increased overall public spending by 25 per cent, public works expenditure rose by 32 per cent and the social welfare budget by 29 per cent, whilst taxes were slashed. This was a sharp break with the previous budgets, all of which had been balanced. The explosion of government spending aroused serious opposition in the LDP but Tanaka was powerful enough to ram it through the cabinet. When the finance minister died the day after presenting the supplementary budget required to pay for the substantial increase in government expenditure, Tanaka was forced to accept his arch-rival, Fukuda, as minister of finance. Fukuda was a former Ministry of Finance bureaucrat and a fiscal conservative, but significantly he too sensed Tanaka was providing the party with essential public support by responding to demands for increased spending on social welfare and public works. The 1974 budget was significant because it

> symbolized as well as anything else the LDP's crossover from being a party of farmers in a developing economy to being the major political voice for a broad range of individuals and groups living in a modern industrial and increasingly postindustrial society. (Curtis, 1988: 65–6)

Tanaka had enjoyed considerable public popularity when he had become prime minister but this rapidly evaporated. His expansionary budgets and plans for the physical renovation of the entire nation, plus monetary policies which injected inflation, had unfortunate effects. Well ahead of the 1973 oil shock, Japan was afflicted by a grim combination of inflation, a rapid increase in land prices caused by speculation and rapidly rising budget deficits. Tanaka's popularity, and therefore his usefulness to the LDP, had plummeted even before he was engulfed by scandal. Tanaka's policies stored up difficult long-term problems for Japan, but his downfall was not the result of misguided economic policies.

The Corrupt Tradition and the Lockheed Scandal

Political corruption and scandal had a long history in modern Japan. The first major scandal came in 1880–1 when the Meiji government sold its assets in Hokkaido at knockdown prices to relatives and associates of the oligarchy which ruled Japan. In 1914 a scandal involving bribes from the Siemens Company brought down the government. During the period of Taishō democracy in the 1920s, there were frequent scandals involving illegal receipt of money by party politicians. There were also numerous allegations of close and corrupt relationships between the various political parties and the *zaibatsu* which the enemies of party government found to be effective weapons against democracy.

The tradition of corruption and scandal continued after the Second World War. In October 1948 the Ashida cabinet fell following allegations of corrupt payments to ministers and bureaucrats by an electricity company. A scandal involving corrupt payments to high-ranking politicians by shipbuilding interests was one of the reasons why Yoshida Shigeru was bundled out of the premiership in 1954. Two of the senior figures arrested in the scandals of 1948 and 1954 but later amnestied, Fukuda Takeo and Satō Eisaku, became prime minister. There were no spectacular instances of corruption and scandal in the 1960s, still there were sufficient instances, minor by Japanese standards, for the latter part of the 1960s to be christened *kuroi kiri* ('black mist'). In the last twenty years of its monopoly of office, the LDP was regularly rocked by ever-larger scandals involving corrupt payments.

The interlinked root causes of the development of 'money politics' which this corruption and scandal represents were the Japanese electoral system and widespread factionalism within the LDP. An LDP candidate for the House of Representatives had to find vast sums of money to get elected because of the nature of the electoral system. With one exception, the country was divided into multi-member constituencies. Most constituencies returned between four and six members but each elector cast only one vote. The LDP invariably ran more than one candidate in each constituency. Consequently, LDP candidates competed not only against opposition party candidates for the total vote but also against fellow LDP members for the LDP vote. To cope with this, LDP politicians created local support groups, known as *koenkai*, whose role was to attract sufficient of the LDP vote to ensure their election. Building the *koenkai* and financing its operations cost immense amounts of money. Few individual politicians could generate sufficient money themselves to finance their own election success. For almost all rank-and-file LDP politicians, the solution to the problem of money was to join a faction whose leader could raise the required funds. Factions were vital to their leaders as means to generate sufficient personal support for them to have a reasonable chance of winning the presidency of the party, and therefore becoming prime minister. A successful faction leader was a successful fund raiser. He rarely bound his faction members to him through ideology or community of political belief, still less by personal charisma. Instead, the prime attraction of a faction leader was as provider of vast, and frequently illicitly acquired, sums of money. Until the period of Tanaka Kakuei's dominance, most factions were relatively small. One of Tanaka's innovations in the LDP was the creation of a very large faction, having the allegiance of well over 100 members. As the size of factions, and especially that of Tanaka, mushroomed, so ever larger amounts of money had to be raised by the leaders. This was the basic reason why the frequency and dimensions of corruption scandals increased after 1970

Tanaka Kakuei inaugurated the era of super-scandals. Tanaka had his first brush with corruption whilst serving his first of many terms in the House of Representatives in 1948 when he was found guilty of taking bribes from coal-mine owners. Tanaka was subsequently acquitted by a higher court and grew into the arch-manipulator of illicit political funding. His former existence as a construction entrepreneur gave him close ties with that industry, which was one of the prime sources of illicit political contributions. Tanaka's skills enabled him to increase his faction and to buy more votes to wage his own campaigns in the interminable LDP internal feuds in the early 1970s. However, his administration became engulfed in a fog of allegations of corrupt payments from real estate and construction interests and in November 1974 he was forced out of the prime ministership. Then in 1976 Tanaka, and the LDP, were engulfed in the Lockheed affair, which dwarfed any previous scandal in postwar Japan.

At the centre of the Lockheed affair in Japan were illicit payments made by the Lockheed Corporation in 1972 to have their TriStar airliner bought by the state-owned All Nippon Airways. In Japan Lockheed's total clandestine payments totalled ¥2.6 billion, of which ¥780 million went to various politicians, including ¥500 million to Tanaka. In February 1976 Lockheed's worldwide activities were revealed in a US Senate investigation and, despite attempts by the US government to prevent leaks, Lockheed's payments in Japan surfaced. On 27 July 1976 Tanaka Kakuei and one of his associates were arrested. The Lockheed scandal was unlike previous affairs in the size of the sums involved, the salacious details of which included the involvement of a former war criminal with links to the *yakuza* – Japan's version of the mafia. On this occasion, unusually, there was a real threat that Lockheed could have serious legal consequences for the politicians involved. Tanaka was tried and, after seven years' deliberation, the Tokyo District Court found him guilty and sentenced him to four years in prison and a heavy fine. In the event, neither sentence was imposed on the errant former prime minister; nor did the LDP take any serious action either to remove the basic reasons for corruption in politics or to clean 'money politics' out of the party (Herzog, 1993).

Musical Prime Ministers 1974–82

As Tanaka's resignation became unavoidable in 1974, two of the titans of the LDP threatened to lock horns in the battle for the presidency of the party. Fukuda Takeo had been Tanaka's victim in the money contest of 1972; Ōhira Masayoshi was the heir of Ikeda Hayato, prime minister between 1960 and 1964. The two contestants, and their supporters, were fairly evenly matched. Against a climate of growing public disgust at political corruption, a presidential election between the two on the scale of 1972, with money politics again on public display, would have been very dangerous at time when the LDP was in electoral difficulties. The intense rivalry between Fukuda and Ōhira raised the distinct possibility that a contest between them could break the party. These factors led the party vice-chairman, and elder statesman, Shiina Etsusaburo, to anoint himself as a mediator and king-maker. His choice fell on Miki Takeo, the leader of a small faction who had an image of incorruptibility. In the circumstances the faction leaders saw the need to allay public fury at the less savoury aspects of the LDP and they meekly accepted Miki, who succeeded Tanaka as prime minister on 9 December 1974 (Hrebenar, 1986).

Miki was a well-known and sincere advocate of reform to curb the abuses of the LPD's finances. He was popularly known as the 'House Cleaning Prime Minister', a play on the Japanese term for prime minister and the word for domestic cleaning. He drew up new regulations for conduct

126

within the party which would have checked the massive illicit injections of cash into the party from big business. Hardly surprisingly, he ran straight into entrenched interests too powerful for him to overcome. Further, there was a compelling argument against radical reform of the rules on political contributions. The LDP's finances were in an appalling state. It still had a ¥10 billion debt from the 1972 election and another general election was imminent and would require further mountains of money. Miki was forced to water down regulations concerning party finance which proved to be 'a very light burden for the LDP–business alliance to bear'. By 1976 the Miki government was increasingly paralysed by the unfolding revelations of the Lockheed scandal and Tanaka Kakuei's deep involvement in it. The scandal itself ultimately had surprisingly little permanent impact upon political processes but did seriously disrupt the Miki administration. Miki refused to use his powers to save Tanaka from the law and this brought down upon him the wrath of the powerful Tanaka faction and its allies. Miki had another problem in having to fight a general election which had to be held in 1976. When the election was held in December 1976 the LDP's share of the popular vote slumped to 41.8 per cent. Against the background of the Lockheed scandal and the problems that had rocked the economy since late 1972, the LDP could have expected little better. In any case, the peculiarities of the electoral system maintained the party's overall majority in the House of Representatives, but the election sealed Miki's fate.

On Christmas Eve 1976 Fukuda Takeo finally achieved his ambition when he succeeded the hapless Miki Takeo as prime minister. Fukuda was the latest in the long line of ex-bureaucrats who had entered conservative politics. As a former senior civil servant in the Ministry of Finance, Fukuda regarded himself as an expert on Japan's economy and intended that his government would concentrate on economic policy. This proved impossible since his administration was constantly dogged by the reverberations of the Lockheed scandal. Fukuda was not a popular prime minister and his position in the LDP was not strong since he attracted the hostility of both the Tanaka and Ōhira factions. In an attempt to reduce their influence and strengthen his own position in the party, Fukuda turned to a proposal originally proposed by Miki Takeo to change the method of chosing the party's president. The new rules for the election of the LDP president introduced a primary election amongst the rank-and-file LDP members and so-called 'party friends'. The two candidates who gained the largest number of votes in this primary election would go on to the second stage of the election in which LDP members of both houses of parliament would vote. Fukuda imagined that the new system for the presidential election would counteract much of the financial power of the rival factions. Ironically, Fukuda was the first victim of this new system. The factions sank their financial tentacles into the grass roots of the party. LDP membership tripled, rising from 500,000 to 1,500,000, many of the subscriptions being paid for by the factions. Effectively, the new electoral system spread factionalism into the local party organisations. Consequently, the cost of competing for the presidency of the party rocketed and increased the factions' need for money. In the presidential election of 1978 Fukuda, the architect of the new arrangements, was simply out-moneyed by Ōhira Masayoshi, supported by the Tanaka faction. He was defeated heavily in the first, primary stage and withdrew from the contest, leaving the road open to Ōhira (Tomita *et al.*, 1986).

Ōhira had become prime minister as a result of his alliance with the Tanaka faction. This stirred the hostility of the ousted Fukuda and his faction, which combined with the Miki faction to snipe continually at Ōhira. Curiously, Fukuda and Ōhira should have been natural allies since both were former Ministry of Finance bureaucrats. Ōhira had been introduced into politics by Ikeda Hayato and had ultimately inherited Ikeda's faction. Ōhira had to deal with an economic situation exacerbated by the second oil shock and constant criticism from Fukuda, who complained of

Ōhira's relationship with the Tanaka faction. In the general election held in October 1979 the LDP fell eight short of a majority in the House of Representatives. Fukuda demanded that Ōhira take responsibility for the electoral defeat and resign, but the prime minister decided to soldier on. When the new parliament convened in November, Fukuda challenged Ōhira for the premiership. The LDP was almost evenly split, so both Ōhira and Fukuda sought support from the opposition parties. At one stage, it seemed possible that Fukuda could get the support of the DSP, an alliance that would have produced a coalition government. Ultimately, however, most of the opposition parties were unwilling to play coalition politics and Ōhira scraped into the premiership with the support of the New Liberal Club, which had broken from the LDP in 1974. This parliamentary contest for the prime ministership raised factional infighting to a new intensity. On 16 May 1980 the Fukuda and Miki factions absented themselves from a routine JSP motion of no-confidence against the Ōhira government and the government was defeated. Ōhira had to call a general election. Ten days before it took place, Ōhira died suddenly. This produced a wave of sympathy which, combined with unusually good weather for late June, increased the LDP vote and gave them a safe majority in both houses of parliament (Hayes, 1992).

The death of Ōhira had been completely unexpected and the faction leaders were unprepared for a presidential contest. Complex horsetrading took place between six LDP factions, with Tanaka Kakuei, who had not been a member of the LDP since 1976, acting as the most influential broker. These manoeuvrings led to the appointment as prime minister of the man who had succeeded as leader of the Ōhira faction, Suzuki Zenkō. The emergence of Suzuki as prime minister raised to new heights the Japanese tradition that senior political office should be held by men of low public profile and no discernible charisma. His major attraction for the faction leaders was that Suzuki was wholly unprepared for office and would be only a temporary incumbent until the major party figures sorted out their future plans (Curtis, 1988).

It seemed likely that the rapid turnover of cabinets and ministers in the decade following Tanaka Kakuei's appointment as prime minister in 1972 would erode the role of politicians in framing and implementing policy and further strengthen the power and influence of the bureaucracy. Unexpectedly, the outcome was rather different and politicians were able to alter the balance of power with the bureaucracy in their own favour. This was the result of Tanaka and his successors encouraging LDP members of parliament to form and develop so-called policy *zoku* (usually translated as 'tribes'). These were groups of LDP politicians who focused on particular areas of policy, thereby building up substantial specialist knowledge on important issues such as agriculture, trade and construction. By the mid-1980s senior bureaucrats were admitting that the LDP politicians in their various *zoku* were at least as influential as themselves in policymaking. As the *zoku* became more sophisticated, politicians and ministers were increasingly able to deal with bureaucrats on equal terms and eroded the bureaucracy's primacy in decision-making from without, whilst conflict between ministries for control of key areas of policymaking weakened civil service power from within (Nester, 1990).

The First 'Oil Shock'

On 16 October 1973, during the latter stages of the Yom Kippur War between Israel and the Arab powers, the Organization of Arab Petroleum Exporting Countries (OAPEC) announced a two-thirds increase in the price of crude oil, from $3 to $5 per barrel. This was closely followed by a complete oil embargo by OAPEC against the United States and progressive cutbacks in the supply of Arab oil to other industrialised countries including Japan; within a month of the imposition of the embargo supplies were down to three-quarters of normal shipments. From November there was a

steady easing of restrictions on Middle Eastern oil supplies
to most European countries but Japan was not included in
this relaxation. It was only after the Japanese government
issued a statement in support of the Arab position in the
Middle Eastern conflict, and the deputy prime minister,
Miki Takeo, had toured the region and made appropriate
pro-Arab noises in December that supplies of Arab oil to
Japan were increased to 85 per cent of pre-embargo figures.
It was not until in March 1974 that restrictions on the supply of Arab oil to Japan were fully lifted (Lincoln, 1988).

Japan's high-speed growth had been heavily dependent
on the use of cheap imported oil and the steep price increases were a heavy blow to the economy. In 1974, after
the OAPEC action, Japan's GNP actually contracted by 1.4
per cent, the first decline in national wealth since the end
of the war. The economy recovered some of its dynamism
but there would be no return to the heady, double-digit
rates of growth experienced in the 1960s. In addition, after
two decades of relatively stable prices, Japan experienced
very high levels of inflation, known as the 'crazy prices',
which reached its zenith in 1974 when the rate of inflation
shot up to 31.6 per cent. It was naturally assumed that
Japan's era of rapid growth had been brought to an end by
the oil shock. However, even before the oil shock other
forces were at work, putting a brake on the rapid growth of
the 1950s and 1960s (Ito, 1992).

At the beginning of the 1970s confidence in the Japanese
economy's prospects both at home and abroad was growing.
In 1972 Tanaka Kakuei, soon to become prime minister,
published his blueprint for the country's future, *Building a
New Japan* [*Nihon Rettō Kaizō Ron*]. This envisaged Japan's
high rate of growth being sustained by a great remodelling
of the country. Tanaka's master plan would deal with pollution and the other consequences of expansion while
spreading the economic 'miracle' to all parts of Japan.
Parallel with the physical remodelling of the economy and
country, a comprehensive social welfare structure would be
created. This twin-track policy would make government

expenditure one of the prime engines of continued growth. At Tanaka's behest, the Economic Planning Agency published an official reworking of the remodelling plans, *Basic Economic and Social Plan: Toward a Vigorous Welfare Society 1973–1977*, which forecast a growth rate of 9 per cent per year, only 2 per cent less than the average between 1961 and 1970 (Lincoln, 1988).

These optimistic forecasts and grandiose plans were throttled by factors working through the economy even before the 1973 oil shock. The end of the Bretton Woods system and revaluation of the yen did create real problems for the economy. Unfortunately, business overestimated the potential impact of these difficulties and government policy overcompensated for them. One great fear was that the yen would float above its new rate of exchange of $1 = ¥308, making Japanese products uncompetitive abroad. The other fear was that there might be a downturn in industrial growth. The government's solution was a rapid increase in the money supply to inject inflation into the domestic economy. This was intended to keep the yen undervalued and stimulate home markets. Even before the oil shock, government policy had produced sharp inflation, and inflationary pressure was fuelled by sharply rising land prices caused by widespread land speculation seeking to profit from Tanaka's remodelling plans (Ito, 1992).

At a more fundamental level, some of the basic factors that had contributed to very rapid rates of growth in manufacturing industry had run their course by the early 1970s. The gap in technology that had existed between Japanese and American and west European industry had all but closed by 1970. In many sectors it was no longer an economic option for Japan to import the most advanced western technology relatively cheaply because it had been developed by Japanese industry itself. The advantage of being technologically a late developer was evaporating and Japanese industry was having to absorb the costs of developing its own cutting-edge technology. Further, most of the advantages of scale that Japanese industry had been building towards in the 1950s and 1960s had been achieved by the early 1970s. In wider society, there was no longer general acceptance of unbridled industrial growth, irrespective of environmental and other costs. In future, industry would have to meet, and deal with, the social costs of its development. These long-term, basic changes in Japan's economic performance were not appreciated in the early 1970s. Hence the government implemented the wrong policies to deal with some of the more superficial difficulties, with consequent harm to the overall economy which, then received a further body blow from the oil shock in the autumn of 1973.

The Economy after the Oil Shock

The 1973 oil crisis hit Japan harder than other industrialised nations because it coincided with internal economic problems and with the end of stability between the world's major currencies. These were developments with which the Japanese economy was ill-equipped to deal. The crisis of 1973–4 traumatised government, business and the general public because it combined the classic symptoms of alarming 'stagflation', recession and inflation. The danger that Japan's oil supplies would be seriously cut revived fears that in the final analysis Japan's economic health was extremely fragile because of the country's total reliance on vital raw materials from outside. The government tried to control the prices of key products by ordinance but this produced damaging distortions in price patterns. Attempts to control petroleum products led to a clash with the international oil companies, who threatened to stop supplying Japan unless they were allowed to pass on the rising prices in crude oils to the Japanese market. Inflation, at 15.7 per cent in 1973, more than doubled to 31.6 per cent by 1974. The sharp, induced recession cut Japan's GNP by 1.4 per cent. This arrested the inflationary spiral and in 1975 prices rose by only 3 per cent (Lincoln, 1988).

The crisis of 1973–4 marked a clear transition point in the structure and nature of the Japanese economy. These changes were not induced by the oil shock alone, for many of the symptoms of transition were present before 1973. The most obvious change was a much slower rate of economic growth after 1973, although it would have happened, more gradually, even without an oil crisis. Hesitantly at first, the growth rate crept up to 4.8 per cent by 1976 and reached 5.3 per cent in 1979 before the second oil shock of that year knocked it back. It was only in 1984 that the economy returned to an annual growth rate of over 5 per cent (actually 5.1 per cent) (Ito, 1992). As the economy recovered, the structure of industry changed. Recovery after 1973 was much more rapid in the tertiary, service, sector than in manufacturing industry, which did not fully recover until 1978. In manufacturing industry there was a rapid shift from the materials industries, such as iron and steel and chemicals, to assembly and knowledge-intensive industries. Between 1975 and 1982 machining and assembly industries grew by 113.7 per cent, whilst basic materials industries grew by a mere 14 per cent. This was a reflection, firstly, of increased energy prices. Materials industries were energy intensive and the rocketing oil prices had a severe impact upon their international price competitiveness. Secondly, it was a consequence of the narrowing technological gap between Japan and the rest of the world in the production of chemicals and steel. The thrust of technological development shifted to numerically controlled machine tools and industrial robots, which were of immense advantage to assembly industries, and assisting knowledge-intensive industries became a government priority (Uekusa, 1988). Finally, the materials-processing industries and heavy industry, such as shipbuilding, began to feel the weight of competition from the newly industrialising countries, such as South Korea and Taiwan. These were economies in which wage levels were far lower than in Japan, and those Japanese industries that were labour intensive found themselves at an increasing disadvantage in world markets.

After 1973 both the government and business saw research and development and technological innovation as the new way of inducing and sustaining economic growth. The closing of the technological gap and changes in the labour force meant that the rate at which business invested declined, and this had the same effect on the rate of increase in productivity and the speed of economic growth. The end of the technological gap in many manufacturing sectors made it less attractive to invest in fresh capital since the returns were diminishing. In addition, the cost of buying in technology rose as Japan came closer to the technological frontier. Investment was also discouraged by a slow down in the rate at which the labour force was improving and therefore the rate at which labour productivity could increase. A greater proportion of the workforce was spending longer in full-time education, improving it qualitatively, but the rate of this qualitative improvement did not match rates in the 1950s and 1960s. Combined with the problem of technology, rates of new investment were curbed by this decline in growth of labour productivity.

In general after 1972–3 the world economy was much less dynamic and supportive of rapid economic growth, though Japan was less affected by this than the other major economies. Before the early 1970s Japanese economic growth had been sustained by the domestic market. Exports played a vital role in generating foreign exchange to buy in raw materials and technology, but the expansion of the economy was based overwhelmingly on satisfying the domestic market. After 1973 the balance between domestic and foreign markets began to alter. Japan generated large balance of payments surpluses, and exports became more important in sustaining growth in the Japanese economy. From 1980 the balance of payments surplus grew very rapidly and the contribution of exports to economic growth soared (Lincoln, 1988). The emergence of Japan's huge balance of payments surpluses, beginning in 1973, had an impact upon politics as great as its economic significance. Japan's gigantic surpluses produced dangerous friction with the United

States and Europe and became an important issue in Japan's domestic politics and international relations in the 1980s and 1990s.

Individual Japanese industries made giant strides after the first oil crisis. The most spectacular example was the automobile industry, the prime specimen of the assembly sector taking full advantage of the changed circumstances after 1973. The severe increase in oil prices raised worldwide concern over fuel conservation and stimulated demand for economical, small cars of the type in which the Japanese automobile industry specialised. The 1973 crisis had also focused public attention on the environmental impact of oil products. To calm the growing tide of disquiet over general environmental pollution in the early 1970s, the Japanese government imposed the world's strictest exhaust emission control laws. When the United States and western Europe tightened their own emission regulations, Japanese manufacturers were in an excellent position to supply vehicles which conformed to these restrictions. By 1976 Japan was exporting 2.5 million vehicles a year, and in 1979 Japan's automobile production overtook that of the United States for the first time. By 1980 automobiles made up 22.7 per cent of the value of Japan's exports (Mutoh, 1988). The nascent Japanese computer industry was also boosted in the 1970s. In 1972 expenditure in Japan on research and development in information technology was US $168 million rising to $300 million the following year, and by 1980 Japan was spending $725 million on developing computer-related technology (Fransmann, 1990). After 1973 Japan became the world leader in robotic machine tools and this gave an enormous boost to productivity in selected industries.

The period 1973–80 was a difficult one for Japan. The political stability of the Ikeda–Satō period had shifted to the turbulence and sleaze of the Tanaka, Fukuda and Ōhira premierships. The Lockheed scandal had lifted the stone of illicit political funding and revealed the seamy underside of LDP dominance. Protestations from politicians that corruption in politics would be stamped out not only came to nothing, but LDP factionalism, at the root of that corruption, also extended into the grass-roots of the party. In the 1980s and 1990s the Japanese political world would be rocked by scandals even greater than Lockheed. High-speed growth had been arrested in 1972–3 and although the economy recovered, the great days of double-digit growth rates were gone. Conversely, the Japanese economy as a whole showed remarkable resilience and flexibility, so that by the time of the second oil shock in 1979 it was on a sound basis. The Japanese people became statistically wealthier, yet many doubted whether their quality of life was improving. The population was deeply stung in 1979 when a European Community report described the Japanese as workaholics living in rabbit hutches. In the 1980s, the quality of life debate joined economic growth and political reform as central issues in Japan.

6

THE EMERGENCE OF THE ECONOMIC SUPERPOWER: 1980 TO THE PRESENT

The second oil shock of 1979–80 did not affect the Japanese economy as severely as the 1973 oil crisis and recovery was fairly rapid. From 1980 to 1990 Japan enjoyed a respectable rate of economic growth, although this was sharply arrested by the onset of a new and unprecedentedly deep recession. In a number of spheres the decade following the second oil shock was one of significant changes and of severe difficulties. From 1982 to 1987, politics was dominated by Nakasone Yasuhiro, a politician who by Japanese standards possessed a charisma of almost unprecedented dimensions. During his five years as prime minister Nakasone set about a number of important domestic reforms and tried to define Japan's role in the world more accurately. Meanwhile, the tainted relationship between Japanese politics and big money spiralled out of control, successive scandals visiting nemesis upon Japanese conservative politics. These scandals, combined with other political and economic difficulties, were responsible for a sea-change in Japan's politics when, in the summer of 1993, the LDP split and lost a monopoly of government that had lasted for nearly four decades.

The Japanese economy continued to grow and by 1987 per capita income in Japan had overtaken that in the United States. A new element in Japan's postwar economic devel-

opment came to prominence after 1980. Much of the returns from continued economic growth were exported for
investment and the purchase of assets abroad. Between
April 1986 and March 1991 total Japanese overseas investment amounted to $227.2 billion and Japan became the
world's largest creditor nation. Japanese investors created
manufacturing bases in North America, Europe and other
parts of Asia. They also bought foreign property, companies, shares and government bonds, notably those of the US
government whose chronic budget deficits were partly
financed by Japanese money. Yet there were dark clouds in
the economic sky. The rise of the newly industrialised
nations in east and south-east Asia, especially South Korea,
threatened competition for key Japanese industries. More
seriously, the status of economic superpower produced
severe difficulties in Japan's relations with the wider world,
particularly with the United States. Japanese–American
relations deteriorated sharply during the 1980s. In large
measure, this was due to a widespread American belief that
Japan was becoming richer at the expense of the United
States. These tensions between Japan and the United States
were exacerbated by the Japanese refusal to take any active
part in the Gulf War in 1991. 'Japan-bashing' became a
popular activity in the US Congress, the American press
and in Hollywood films. For their part, Japanese politicians
made insensitive racial remarks which antagonised American public opinion. The end of the Cold War, with the
disintegration of the Soviet Union, served to divert attention for a time from this deterioration in US–Japanese
relations. Alarmingly, some Americans began to substitute
the Japanese for the Russians as the United States' main
potential foe.

Subtle, and not so subtle, changes were also discernible
in Japanese society. The belief emerged, as the Japanese
people became statistically richer, that most Japanese were
not enjoying the full fruits of economic success. Japanese
living and working conditions were compared unfavourably

with those in Europe and North America, where economic success had been less marked. The Japanese also began to wrestle with the problem of an increasingly ageing society, in which the old would become an ever greater proportion of the population, thus placing a growing burden on an economically active but shrinking segment of the population. By 2025 it was calculated that the economically active proportion of the population would have to pay 35 per cent of their gross income to support pensions, compared to 14 per cent in 1990. Japan also experienced a symbolic change when the Emperor Hirohito died on 7 January 1989, bringing to an end the Shōwa era which had begun in 1926.

Nakasone Yasuhiro and the Politics of Economic Greatness

On 27 November 1982 Nakasone Yasuhiro succeeded the colourless Suzuki Zenkō as prime minister. Nakasone was a veteran politician, having entered politics as a conservative in 1947. From 1967, when he had inherited one of the smaller LDP factions, he had held a bewildering variety of ministerial posts. Nakasone had been associated with Tanaka Kakuei since the late 1960s when Tanaka had been Satō Eisaku's faction manager. Tanaka had received vital support from Nakasone in his battle with Fukuda Takeo for the leadership of the LDP in 1972, and it was therefore natural that Nakasone should support Tanaka in his perpetual conflicts with Fukuda in the 1970s. Nakasone and Fukuda both represented the same multi-member constituency in Gunma, north of Tokyo, and were therefore rivals for the LDP vote in that constituency; in addition, they personally disliked each other. Nakasone's reward for the help he had given Tanaka was vital support for his political career from the great political operator. In Tanaka's 1972 cabinet Nakasone received the influential post of minister for international trade and industry. Thanks again to

Tanaka's support, Nakasone served in the powerful office of secretary-general of the LDP. Nakasone used his opportunities well. As secretary-general of the ruling party he was at the centre of money politics and he used his position to forge powerful political alliances, developing the means of tapping sources of money for his political ambitions. When Suzuki bowed out in 1982 Nakasone's own faction on its own was too small to bring him the leadership but his long association with Tanaka brought him the king-maker's support. With Tanaka's help Nakasone amassed the necessary electoral support to win the premiership. The relationship between the two was so close that the early period of Nakasone's premiership was popularly known as 'Tanakasone rule' (Horsley and Buckley, 1990).

Like Tanaka, Nakasone did not cut the normal figure of an LDP politician. Unlike most postwar politicians, Nakasone had charisma and was a good public speaker, capable of swaying an audience with his eloquence. He skilfully exploited radio and television to build his popular support. At the high point of Nakasone's premiership the LDP enjoyed unprecedented popularity; according to opinion polls the party was supported by more than 57 per cent of the electorate, five points above the previous high. Most of the party's popularity was due to Nakasone's personal standing. In sharp contrast to most Japanese conservative politicians, Nakasone had expressed strong beliefs and a serious political agenda. Above all he was an ardent nationalist who was always anxious to assert Japan's independence. At the beginning of his political career Nakasone had made his mark by criticising the occupation and subsequently he consistently campaigned against aspects of the occupation reforms. He strove to be a 'presidential' prime minister who would exercise real authority from the top rather than being a channel through which passed the ideas and policies of other ministers and of the bureaucracy. He initiated an extensive and effective programme of privatisation, although his attempts at radical reform in education and taxation were not blessed with success (Hayao, 1993). Unlike Japan's previous, and subsequent, prime ministers, Nakasone cut a dash on the international scene, revelling in – rather than avoiding – a positive role at international gatherings. He even succeeded in establishing a reasonably friendly, personal relationship with President Reagan who was rather charmed by the relatively open, and surprisingly tall, Japanese prime minister. Nevertheless, Nakasone did not neglect the necessities of domestic and LDP politics. He was one of the few postwar Japanese prime ministers who became popular during his term of office and he used that popularity to remain in office for five years, thereby temporarily breaking the two-year cycle of faction leader succeeding faction leader as prime minister (Curtis, 1988). He skilfully used his position as prime minister to build a more powerful position within the party. In 1981 the Nakasone faction had only fifty-two members; after his triumph in the 1986 general election Nakasone's faction was second only to the Tanaka faction, with eighty-seven members. To build and maintain this faction. Nakasone continued to use money politics, raising ¥507 million of legal contributions in 1984; the size of the less legal contributions is unknown.

Nakasone was deeply committed to so-called 'administrative reform', a euphemism for overhauling Japan's tax system and privatising state-owned industries and corporations. His motive was to reduce the chronic budget deficit that had afflicted the Japanese government in the late 1970s. Taking his cue from the Thatcher government's privatisation policies in Britain, Nakasone succeeded in taking the major nationalised industries out of government control. In April 1985 the Japan Telegraph and Telephone Corporation (NTT) was privatised. In April 1987 the Japan National Railways, the greatest industrial drain upon government finances, was split up and prepared for sale, and in November 1987 Japan Air Lines (JAL) was placed in the private sector. Although Nakasone achieved most of his objectives in privatising state enterprises, his tax reforms became

bogged down and all but sank in a mire of political opposition, and he made virtually no progress in liberalising the
education system (Hayao, 1993). Nakasone was able to
dilute the influence of article IX of the constitution. In
1984 his government ended the ban on the export of arms
and related goods, a measure that had been a symbolic
obstacle to further Japanese rearmament. He also agreed
to Japanese involvement in President Reagan's Strategic
Defense Initiative, the so-called Star Wars Project. Then
in 1987 Nakasone breached the convention that Japan's
defence expenditure should not exceed 1 per cent of GNP.
Nakasone was not able to accomplish his ultimate aim of
abolishing article IX but he did loosen its hold on Japanese
security and defence policy.

During the early phase of his premiership Nakasone's
position in the LDP was not strong and his parliamentary
position deteriorated severely because of the turbulence
caused by the progress of Tanaka Kakuei's trial. In October
1983 Tanaka was finally found guilty of taking bribes from
the Lockheed Corporation and was sentenced to four years'
imprisonment and fined ¥500 million. The opposition parties deadlocked parliament in an attempt to have Tanaka
expelled, an essential preliminary to the court's sentence being executed. It was soon obvious that the only solution to
this parliamentary stalemate was a general election. The
general election of December 1983 was fought on the issue
of political morality, the least favourable ground for the
LDP. The party uncharacteristically made a serious error in
its electoral arithmetic and put up too many candidates in
the multi-member constituencies. The result was a serious
LDP reverse. Their popular vote went down by 2 per cent
and they fell six short of a majority in the House of Representatives. Nakasone was forced to rely on support from the
New Liberal Club and independents. One member of the
New Liberal Club entered the cabinet, the first non-LDP
politician to do so since the foundation of the party in 1955.
The 1983 general election was a severe reverse for the LDP

but paradoxically it strengthened rather than weakened Nakasone. His faction, and that of his mentor, Tanaka, lost relatively fewer members than did their opponents' factions. The difficult parliamentary situation which the general election produced discouraged the worst excesses of factional infighting within the party. Finally, the party would have to rebuild its popular image if it were to survive the next election, and the skills of the still-popular Nakasone were central to this task.

Nakasone's personal stock continued to rise with the growth of Japan's economy, whilst the confused situation in the LDP further bolstered his position. Within Tanaka Kakuei's faction, Takeshita Noboru, Tanaka's natural successor, had become restive at his failure to obtain the premiership. In early 1985 Takeshita established a 'study group' within Tanaka's faction, the familiar prelude to an attempt to seize control. Shortly afterwards, Tanaka had two severe strokes, reportedly brought on by a paroxysm of anger at Takeshita's action. Tanaka refused to relinquish his grip on his faction, although physically barely capable of political or any other activity. His political days were clearly numbered, but Takeshita needed time and support to ensure that he inherited the bulk of the Tanaka faction. Therefore, he not only left Nakasone alone but supported him in his schemes. Nakasone, meanwhile, used his strengthening position in the LDP to decide on the most opportune time to call a general election. Capitalising on his own personal popularity, and exploiting the economy's strength, Nakasone led the LDP to a decisive victory in a general election n July 1986. The LDP received its largest popular vote since 1963, winning 300 seats in the House of Representatives and enjoying a majority of forty-four. The New Liberal Club, which had broken away from the LDP in 1974, suffered an electoral catastrophe of such dimensions that its parliamentary remnants rejoined the LDP immediately after the election.

Nakasone hoped to take advantage of his stunning electoral victory to extend his period of office, which was due to end in November 1986. He demonstrated consummate skill in navigating the complexities of faction politics and he carefully checked and balanced his potential rivals in the cabinet and the LDP. Nakasone cleverly calmed factional infighting by keeping senior politicians in the same ministerial posts for long periods. Between 1982 and 1986 he placated two of his most serious potential rivals by retaining Abe Shintarō as foreign minister and Takeshita Noboru as finance minister. As leader of the largest LDP faction and king-maker, Tanaka Kakuei had prepared a blueprint for the succession to Nakasone. The premiership would go first to Miyazawa Kiichi, then to Abe Shintarō and finally to the second in command of his faction, Takeshita Noboru. Under this plan, Takeshita would have to wait until at least 1990 to become prime minister. A new generation of politicians were emerging in the LDP and it was not improbable that these younger men would leapfrog over Takeshita and that he would be cheated out of his turn as premier. In the summer of 1986 Takeshita needed more time to prepare his plans to seize control of the largest faction in the LDP. The time was not right for him to challenge Nakasone and he acquiesced in Nakasone's period of office being extended by one year (Reading, 1992).

Nakasone would be prime minister only until autumn 1987 and the powerful men behind the curtains began to jockey for position. Nakasone hoped to use his last year in office to accomplish one of his most cherished ambitions, reform of Japan's taxation system. The premier had first began to pressure for tax reform in 1984. Nakasone had a variety of reasons for his concern with the taxation system. He wished to redress an imbalance in Japan's tax system that had developed since it had been put in place in 1950. Direct taxes had become an increasing element in the government's revenue, whilst indirect taxation had declined. The burden of direct taxation fell disproportionately on middle-class professional families subject to pay-as-you-earn income tax. The urban middle classes were, of course, the essential pillar of the LDP's electoral success. Nakasone and other enthusiasts for tax reform had a much more far-reaching reason for renovating Japan's revenue system. Japan had the world's fastest-ageing population. By 1990 11.7 per cent of Japan's population would be over 65; by 2025 it was estimated that the figure would reach 24 per cent. Care of this growing proportion of old people would fall upon that dwindling proportion of the population which was economically active. The tax reformers argued that Japan ought to change its tax system to generate the revenue necessary for financing a new welfare system to provide for its ageing population. In the 1986 election campaign Nakasone had appeared to promise not to make radical tax increases and after his victory he set about some modest reforms. Nakasone wanted to increase the share of state revenue coming from indirect taxation, thus relieving the payers of income tax. He was interested in a sales tax, such as value-added tax (VAT) but, as a lame-duck prime minister, his position was weak and the powerful Ministry of Finance was able to overcome the prime minister's resistance. VAT immediately provoked widespread popular hostility and opposition both within the LDP and from the other parties in parliament. Nakasone was not able to push through his tax reforms before he ceased to be prime minister on 6 November 1987.

Recruit and Other Scandals

The LDP faction leaders began to stake their claims to the premiership as Nakasone's term drew to a close. Their ambitions threatened an unsavoury contest but this was checked by changes in the balance of factional strength. In July 1987 Takeshita moved against the incapacitated Tanaka and won the loyalty of 113 out of 141 members of the Tanaka faction. He was now the leader of the largest faction, but both Abe and Miyazawa, leaders of the other two largest factions, intended to fight for the party presidency and the premiership. Nakasone and his eighty-three-strong faction held the balance. The LDP chose consensus politics. A deal was arranged giving Takeshita a two-year term as prime minister, after which Abe and Miyazawa would each have their turn for two years.

Nakasone had chosen Takeshita as his successor partly because Takeshita seemed sufficiently strong to push through tax reform. This policy was extremely unpopular, although this was not the only reason why Takeshita was denied a tranquil period of office. The repercussions of the Lockheed scandal had rumbled on into the 1980s, as the leaders of the LDP strove to deal with the embarrassment of Tanaka Kakuei who was still acting as the leader of the largest faction in the party and in a very real sense the king-maker despite being indicted on criminal charges and not even a member of the party. Just when it seemed that the Tanaka problem had been laid to rest, the LDP was rocked by another scandal which, at least in the amount of money involved, dwarfed Lockheed. The Recruit scandal which broke in September 1988 had its origins in a publishing and property company – Recruit Cosmo – throwing money at influential politicians as part of ˙ s strategy to become a major force in the Japanese economy. The LDP, and the factions within it, needed money in the mid-1980s both to fight an impending general election and to finance the intra-party intrigues surrounding the search for a successor to Nakasone. Hence, much of the money that Recruit Cosmo was distributing at the time was sucked into the LDP. The Recruit company used a complicated preferential share mechanism to funnel illegal funds into the ruling party and its factions. Once revelations began to percolate into the public domain, heads began to roll. The scandal's first major victim, in November 1988, was the finance minister, Miyazawa Kiichi, who had illegally received a substantial block of preferential Recruit Cosmo shares. As the tentacles of the scandal spread through the higher reaches of the

LDP Takeshita resolutely proclaimed his innocence, but by April 1989 his position had became intolerable. He was forced to admit that he had 'overlooked' ¥151 million ($1.2 million) received illicitly from Recruit Cosmo. Takeshita stayed on long enough to steer the budget through parliament and resigned on 2 June.

All of the major LDP figures were either involved, or likely to be implicated, in Recruit or one of the lesser scandals that now surfaced. It was no longer possible to honour the succession plans prepared in 1987 according to which the faction leaders would succeed each other as prime minister. The party needed a prime minister whose hands were clean and who could hold the ring until the scandals settled and were forgotten. The faction leaders would then return to their timetable for the prime ministership. Takeshita's successor as premier was the little-known Uno Sousuke, whose main attribute was that he had not been named in the Recruit affair. Uno's short term of office was difficult. The government's tax reforms combined with the consequences of Recruit to produce the first defeat for the LDP in a rural by-election and then the loss of the LDP majority in the House of Councillors following an election on 23 July 1989. Uno had also been tarred by a bizarre scandal concerning a past affair with a *geisha*. Within six weeks of entering office, Uno had to resign. Again, the LDP needed a leader who would not be sucked into scandal – a requirement that ruled out the faction leaders. The calculations were extremely complex, involving not only labyrinthine factional politics but also considerations of age. An older generation of LDP politicians feared that younger hopefuls would seize the premiership and deny them their turn. The choice fell on Kaifu Toshiki. At fifty-eight Kaifu was relatively young but from the point of view of the older conservative leaders he had the great attraction that he did not control a faction and therefore was unlikely to present a generational challenge to Abe, Miyazawa and the other, older hopefuls. He had been closely allied with Miki Takeo, the would-be cleaner of Japanese politics, in the 1970s and this gave Kaifu relatively pure credentials. Kaifu proved more able, and more popular, than had been expected. Public memory of Recruit faded quickly and Kaifu won a respectable majority in the House of Representatives election held in February 1990. Nevertheless, Kaifu's term of office was due to end in October 1991 and aspirants began their intrigues for office.

The usual competition between factions was complicated by the growing contest between generations in the LDP. The up-and-coming younger politicians of the 'Showa' generation, who had been born after 1926, posed a growing challenge to the 'Taishō' generation, who had been born between 1912 and 1926. Kaifu's domestic difficulties arising from the machinations of his would-be successors were compounded by the international complications posed by the Iraqi invasion of Kuwait and the Gulf War between August 1990 and March 1991. Kaifu came under intense pressure from the United States to take some part in the conflict but he could not deliver direct Japanese involvement, although he did manage to obtain a large Japanese contribution to the cost of allied intervention against Iraq.

By 1991 politics within the LDP had become complicated to the point of confusion. In 1990 Takeshita, who had seized Tanaka's faction in 1987, found himself increasingly upstaged within his faction by Kanemaru Shin. The latter was set to become king-maker in 1991, acting through his protégé Ozawa Ichirō. The death in May 1991 of Abe Shintarō, the favourite to succeed Kaifu, further clouded the issue. Also Kaifu had not abandoned hope of winning a second term. In early June, Kaifu took advantage of yet another scandal, this time involving relations between securities (stockbroking) companies, politicians and the *yakuza* (gangster organisations), to launch his campaign to win the LDP presidency for a second term.

Kaifu fought on a platform of radical reform of Japan's electoral system and control over political donations. Political reform had been a regular refrain in the midst of each scandal but hitherto nothing effective had been done. Kaifu's proposals would have ended Japan's multi-member constituency system and could have ended money politics and curbed the power of the faction leaders. Hardly surprisingly these politicians blocked Kaifu's reforms. By 1991 all public opinion polls made Kaifu Japan's most popular postwar prime minister, outstripping Nakasone, but he did not get a second term. In the horse-trading that followed, Miyazawa Kiichi, who had been forced to resign as finance minister during the Recruit scandal, became prime minister on 5 November 1991.

The Political Mould Cracks

Miyazawa's succession marked the return of the older LDP generation. He was seventy-two years old in 1991 and came from the bureaucratic tradition of the LDP, having been a senior official in the Ministry of Finance before being brought into politics by Ikeda Hayato. Miyazawa was a fluent English speaker who had many contacts in the United States and Europe and there were great hopes for him in the international arena. Domestically, Miyazawa was tied to the Takeshita faction and to Kanemaru on whom he had been forced to rely during the leadership contest. This rapidly became clear when six of the twenty-one members of Miyazawa's cabinet were drawn from Takeshita's faction, compared with four from Miyazawa's faction.

Miyazawa had a deeply unhappy term of office. He was dogged by controversy over Japan's relations with the United States, especially the issue of permitting foreign rice to be imported into Japan, by the growing repercussions of the economic recession and, particularly, by a new round of scandals. The scandals, and Miyazawa's failure to legislate political reforms intended to end them, led not only to the fall of the prime minister but also to something close to a revolution in postwar politics. The first victim was Kanemaru Shin, Miyazawa's backer. In August 1992 Kanemaru admitted that he had received ¥500 million from a transport company that had given large illegal contributions to politicians. Kanemaru was forced to resign from parliament, although he received only a derisory legal punishment. He reappeared in the centre of the political stage in March 1993 when investigators raided his office and found ¥1 billion worth of concealed gold which had been acquired to avoid tax.

Miyazawa had great difficulty in pushing through any reform to end the scandals. In a move which received little attention at the time, Hosokawa Morihiro, the governor of Kumamoto prefecture in Kyushu, set up the Japan New Party (JNP), which was dedicated to serious political reform. The JNP had some success in the election for the House of Councillors held in July 1992. Following the second Kanemaru scandal, a television interviewer trapped Miyazawa into promising political reform. Again, Miyazawa was unable to overcome the resistance of the faction leaders to any kind of effective reform. In November 1992 there had been a defection of forty-four members from the Takeshita faction and this proved to be a prelude to mass desertion from the LDP itself. A number of politicians of the younger generation began to defect from the LDP, forming two independent parties, *Shinseitō* (Japan Renewal Party) and *Shintō Sakigake*, translated loosely as the New Harbinger Party. These defectors from the LDP voted with the opposition to defeat Miyazawa in a no-confidence motion on 18 June 1993. Miyazawa was forced to call a general election in which, when it was held on 18 July, the LDP fell more than thirty seats short of a majority in the House of Representatives. After a labyrinthine series of negotiations, a seven-party coalition of opposition parties was put together, led by the Hosokawa Morihiro whose year-old Japan Renewal Party had won thirty-five seats. On 8 August 1993 Hosokawa became the first non-LDP prime minister since

1955. The new coalition government was committed to reform designed to transform the political system which had operated in Japan since 1955.

The formation of the Hosokawa cabinet was the start of a period of instability, indeed confusion, unparalleled in postwar Japanese politics. The coalition itself was an unwieldy beast. The seven parties who were its creators ranged across the whole political spectrum, from the right-wing defectors from the LDP to the hard left of the JSP. Hosokawa committed himself to achieving political reform, the customary euphemism for changing the electoral system and curbing money politics, by the end of the year. Unfortunately for the new prime minister, the vested interests of the various coalition parties meant that they had different views of what shape the new electoral system should take. Electoral arithmetic dictated that the defectors from the LDP favoured a system heavily slanted towards single-member constituencies, whilst the smaller parties, and particularly the JSP, pressed for proportional representation. The confusion was compounded by internal divisions over political reform in the LDP, which was now the main opposition party. Of course, Japan's ordinary political, economic and international problems did not go into hibernation whilst the new government wrestled with the complexities of coalition government. The Hosokawa cabinet was faced with the worst economic downturn in Japan since the late 1940s. The government was preoccupied with maintaining its own unity and trying to produce a consensus on political reform, and the economic crisis was neglected. The United States continued to apply pressure on Japan to liberalise and deregulate its economy. One of the main points of focus of this US pressure caused acute difficulties for the coalition government. The Americans had long demanded that Japan permit the import of foreign rice. The problem for Hosokawa was that the principal supporters of maintaining the ban on rice imports were the JSP and the LDP, both of which relied heavily on support in rural Japan. Ominously, therefore, the largest party in the coalition and the largest opposition party shared a common view on a key policy issue.

The political reform bill, which provided for a mixed electoral system of single-member constituencies and proportional representation and a curb on political contributions, passed the House of Representatives on 18 November 1993 but soon got bogged down in the House of Councillors, when it became hopelessly enmeshed with disputes over taxation and rice imports. Not only did Hosokawa fail to fulfil his promise to pass the bill before the end of the year, but when it was finally extricated from the mess into which it had fallen and passed through the House of Councillors on 21 January 1994, it did so in a watered down form and only with the support of the LDP. This seriously damaged Hosokowa's public image since it gave the impression that he had compromised on his principles. Worse was to follow. In March 1994 the LDP began seriously to obstruct the budget to extort an explanation of some shady financial dealings in which Hosokowa was alleged to have been involved in 1982. On 8 April 1994 Hosokawa resigned to 'take responsibility' for his past financial dealings – which somewhat bizarrely concerned the gates on his house – and for the general failings of his cabinet.

After protracted negotiations Hata Tsutomu of the Japan Renewal Party was appointed prime minister on 25 April. Later that day the JSP, alleging that the right-wing parties were forming a new political grouping which excluded them, deserted the coalition, in which it was the largest party. On 29 April Hata was able to announce his cabinet; it was the first minority government in Japan since 1948. On 24 June 1994 parliament eventually passed the budget, which was regarded as essential in helping to drag the Japanese economy out of its depression. This was immediately followed by the LDP, this time in alliance with the JSP, threatening to mount a vote of no confidence against the Hata cabinet. Hata resigned the next day and after four days of negotiations of the utmost tortuousness and cynicism, Murayama Tomiichi, the leader of the JSP, became the first non-conservative prime minister since Katayama Tetsu in 1948. Murayama, who had of course never held government office, was a figure from the left of the JSP; the principal partner in the new coalition, and the party which supplied the majority of the new cabinet, was the LDP.

The Giant in the International Economy

In 1979 the Japanese economy was hit by another increase in oil prices. This time the cost of oil merely doubled; in 1973–4 the price had risen fivefold. None the less, industry and the economy received a sharp jolt. By 1979, of course, oil prices were much higher than they had been in 1973 and the consequences of a doubling were substantial. Japan had one advantage over most other industrialised economies: it had been transformed into the world's most efficient energy-using nation by measures introduced after the first oil shock to save on oil imports. In the 1960s, imports of energy had accounted for around 3 per cent of GNP, but by 1984 this had been cut to 1.6 per cent (Emmott, 1989). The effect of the second oil crisis on Japan's economic development was less drastic than the first, which had actually contributed to an absolute decline in Japan's national wealth. The second oil shock essentially cut back the rate of growth of the economy. Thus, in 1979 Japan's GNP had grown by 5.3 per cent, but this was knocked back to 3.7 per cent in 1980 and the economy did not return to 5 per cent growth until 1984 (Lincoln, 1988).

Exports proved to be an important source of economic recovery for Japan. Between April 1979 and April 1980 Japanese car exports increased by 50 per cent and it has been calculated that four-fifths of Japan's growth in 1980 came from exports. This proportion declined appreciably in subsequent years but even in 1985 exports were responsible for one-fifth of the increase in Japan's GNP. Japan's buoyant export trade depended on a seriously undervalued yen, which made Japanese exports relatively cheap abroad. This monetary advantage was boosted in the early 1980s by the rapid rise in the value of the US dollar, caused by the Reagan administration's fiscal policies. As Japan's exports rose rapidly, Japanese trade and trade practices assumed a high international profile. In May 1981 the Japanese had been pressured into voluntary limits on automobile exports. Outside pressure built up on Japan to correct the growing foreign account surpluses by changing Japanese business and trading methods, and even to accomplish this by restructuring the economy. There was an intensely political dimension to this economic friction since it brought confrontation with the United States.

Trouble with the Outside World

The United States was postwar Japan's most important trading partner whilst Japan was second only to Canada in US foreign trade. Trade friction between the United States and Japan had a long history, starting in 1959, when there were complaints about the large quantities of transistor radios being exported by the Japanese (Tsuru, 1993). In the 1960s and 1970s there were squabbles between the United States and Japan over textiles, steel, television sets and machine tools. These disputes usually began with US manufacturers complaining about the growth in imports of a particular product from Japan. Negotiations between the US and Japanese governments would follow and some quotas or price fixing would be agreed. The disputes after 1980 were of a different order to these earlier spats. They concerned broader issues and threatened much more serious consequences.

The massive increase in Japan's trade surpluses with the United States was at the root of this economic strife. Many American politicians and commentators argued that these surpluses were the result of Japan's unfair trading practices, that foreigners did not have a 'level playing field' in their economic relations with the Japanese, and that underhand practices were damaging or destroying important American industries. Initially this economic friction seemed destined to follow the familiar pattern. The rapid rise in Japanese vehicle exports in 1979–80 caused alarm in other automobile manufacturing countries, but none more so that the United States where the automobile industry had the status of a national symbol and where, more immediately, the Chrysler Corporation was on the verge of bankruptcy. Washington negotiated voluntary export restraints on Japanese automobile exports to the United States and these restricted the flow between 1981 and 1984 to 1.68 million per year. Subsequent agreements increased these quotas and after 1986 the Japanese unilaterally imposed a quota of 2.3 million vehicles, although in reality the figure was only around 1.8 million (Ito, 1992).

The rapid growth of a huge general Japanese trade surplus between 1984 and 1987 changed the nature of the friction between Japan and the United States and the form of solution which the latter demanded. In 1985 Japan had a trade surplus of $49.2 billion and by 1987 this had grown to $87 billion; in 1987 the United States had a deficit of $52 billion in its trade with Japan. Before the Plaza Agreement in September 1985, in which the major economic powers agreed to help devalue the dollar, the US currency was grossly overvalued. This meant that Japanese goods were relatively cheap in the United States and contributed to the very strong American demand for Japanese consumer and other goods. A considerable proportion of Japan's massive surpluses were therefore amassed at the expense of the United States. Initially the Reagan administration was not very critical of the Japanese but the Democrat-dominated Congress was much more strident. In March 1985 Japan was named as 'an unfair trading partner' by the Senate. At first, American fire was concentrated on specific Japanese exports, particularly in electronics and automobiles, and US pressure persuaded the Japanese government to conciliate.

In the mid-1980s American demands shifted from simple quotas and artificial pricing agreements to insistence that the structure of Japan's economy be reformed since its existing form meant that the Japanese were trading unfairly. The US criticisms ranged wide. They condemned the high level of Japanese saving because it cut that consumer spending which might have resulted in the import of American goods. The Americans claimed that the Japanese retail distribution system was so complex and exclusionary that most US suppliers of consumer goods were quite unable to penetrate into it. Restrictions on building large-scale retail outlets were blamed for the failure of large American chain stores to open branches in Japan. This led to the plight of the Toys-'R-Us chain in Japan becoming an issue at the highest levels of government. The relationship between different segments of the *keiretsu*, the large conglomerates, was criticised because of preferential loans and trading conditions which existed between them. The Japanese construction industry was held responsible for the inability of US firms to share in large building projects. A curious, though central, American criticism was that the Japanese worked too hard, making them more productive whilst also limiting the leisure time during which they could become consumers of US goods. In sum, the Americans argued that the prized 'level playing field' in US–Japanese trade could be achieved only by fundamental structural reform deep within Japan's economy.

To an extent, the Japanese were co-operative. Nakasone set up a special commission under Maekawa Haruo, and in April 1986 its report recommended some changes, albeit vague, in Japanese economic institutions. The Nakasone government urged their countrymen to buy foreign goods and Japanese monetary policy between 1985 and 1987 was largely devoted to making the yen appreciate against the dollar, making Japanese exports to the United States more expensive and American goods in Japan cheaper. In March

1985 the dollar stood at ¥260; by February 1987 this had been almost halved to ¥140. This policy of *endaka*, a high-valued yen, worked on the trade surplus. In 1988 it was reduced to $79.6 billion, down from $87 billion the previous year, and by 1990 the surplus had been cut to $35.8 billion. The explosion in the value of the yen, however, had a negative effect and served to open a new front in Japanese–American economic tensions. *Endaka* made US companies and property relatively much cheaper to Japanese corporations and individuals. High-profile Japanese purchases of prominent properties, such as the Rockefeller Centre, which was bought by a Mitsubishi subsidiary in 1989, or Japanese acquisition of American cultural icons, such as the Columbia Picture Corporation, which Sony acquired also in 1989, raised the emotional temperature in the United States (Emmott, 1993). In Japan, some conservative politicians reacted by trying to whip up nationalist fervour against the United States. One of them, Ishihara Shintaro, sold one million copies of his bluntly titled book *The Japan That Can Say No* (Ishihara, 1991).

This economic friction spilt into the political dimensions of US–Japanese relations. The Americans had long believed that the Japanese were getting 'a free ride' from the US security system. Article IX of the constitution, which had legally demilitarised Japan, had been circumvented since 1950 but still it remained a political ideal that Japan should not spend more than 1 per cent of its GNP on defence. Nakasone had managed to break through the 1 per cent barrier. By the 1980s Japan had one of the world's largest defence budgets but successive governments interpreted the constitution as preventing the use of the Self-Defence Forces outside Japan. The end of the Cold War reduced Japan's strategic importance to the United States, whilst the Iraqi invasion of Kuwait in August 1990 and the Gulf War at the beginning of 1991 reinforced the American suspicion that the United States was, without reward, defending vital Japanese economic interests throughout the world. The

Japanese were inveigled into paying much of the cost of the Gulf War but the impression of a free ride in the Gulf fed the Japan-bashers. The inconsequential visit of President George Bush to Japan in January 1991, the most notable incident of which was the president vomiting over Prime Minister Miyazawa, sharpened criticism of Japan by US politicians who were gearing up for the 1992 presidential campaign. The incoming Democrat administration of Bill Clinton proved less stridently anti-Japanese than had been feared in Tokyo. Never the less, US pressure for the economic 'level playing field' was kept up as the Japanese economy plunged into its worst crisis since 1952.

The 'Bubble Economy' and Deep Economic Crisis

During the second half of the 1980s the Japanese domestic economy was awash with money. This liquidity financed high levels of company investment, and thereby sustained economic growth, maintained high levels of foreign direct investment, and bought foreign bonds and securities. The reservoir of cash also sustained the so-called 'bubble economy' in which banks loaned huge sums to finance the purchase of land and shares. It seemed that Japan was immune to the economic woes of the rest of the world. When the world's major stock markets crashed in October 1987 shares on the Tokyo market did fall by 15 per cent in one day but they then steadied and the market resumed its seemingly unstoppable rise. Land prices spiralled upwards whilst the Tokyo Stock Exchange experienced an explosion in share prices, which increased by 120 per cent between October 1987 and December 1989. Companies, corporations and individuals used their holdings of land and shares, which had vastly inflated in value, to borrow more to buy more land and shares. Bank investment in property companies doubled land and property prices between 1986 and 1989. Japan experienced an unprecedented boom in consumer spending, much of it financed through credit. Domestic capital investment, heavy consumer spending and the 'bubble economy' sustained high levels of economic growth. This economic growth sucked imports into Japan, temporarily relieving some of the international pressure to restructure Japan's trading practices and economic structures.

The façade of Japan's immunity to world economic trends crumbled when the 'bubble economy' burst in 1989. Much of the economy's growth had been founded on vast increases in the value of shares, property and land which was not supported by facts. When reality dawned in 1989 the Tokyo Stock Market lost 48 per cent of its share values in the first half of the year. A steady decline in land prices left property companies, plus the banks that had financed them, with assets whose value was much reduced. The commercial banks found themselves with huge loans which were unlikely to be repaid. The eleven main Japanese banks accrued bad debts of perhaps ¥20,000 billion. Many ordinary Japanese hit by the decline in the share market had run up large debts during the period of high consumer spending. Such big spending declined rapidly as a result of a slowdown in the rate of increase in income, from 8.3 per cent in 1990 to 3.2 per cent in 1992, and as the rate of savings increased as families tried to rebuild their finances. This fall in demand in the domestic market was accompanied by a decline in demand for Japanese goods abroad, due largely to the rise in the value of the yen, which made Japanese goods more expensive. The automobile industry, which employed 10 per cent of the industrial workforce and accounted for 13 per cent of industrial production, experienced a 16 per cent fall in demand between the summer of 1991 and August 1992. By the summer of 1993 the economy was in serious recession, threatened with a real decline in GNP. It was against this grim economic background that the political upheavals already discussed took place. Recovery from this unparalleled economic trough was painfully slow and only in the third quarter of 1994 was it clear that the economy was beginning to grow again.

The certainties of Japanese political, economic and even social life were threatened by developments in the five years before 1993. A combination of economic recession and outrage at continued scandal ended the LDP's monopoly of power in August 1993, although the resulting government was a potentially unstable, seven-party coalition. The economy fell into recession in 1990–1 and by 1993 commentators were ruminating on the collapse of the Japanese banking system and the end of the lifetime employment system. Japan's most important ally, the United States, increasingly demanded fundamental changes in the structure of the Japanese economy. By the early 1990s one of the most debated social phenomena was *karoshi*, death from overwork. Life as an economic superpower had become truly complicated.

CONCLUSION

In August 1945 a shattered Japan had surrendered uncondi-
tionally. Only a reckless soothsayer would have prophesied
that Japan's economy would become the postwar era's most
successful and grow into the world's second largest. By 1990
Japan's per capita GNP was the highest of the major
industrial economies. Japanese overseas assets were unprecedentedly large and Japanese goods had a worldwide
reputation second to none. This astonishing growth had
fundamentally changed the structure of Japanese society. In
1950 48.3 per cent of the working population made their
living in primary industry, principally agriculture. By 1992
official statistics put the proportion of the workforce in
agriculture at 6.7 per cent, although it is believed that the
real figure is closer to 3 per cent. Japan had become a
predominantly urban society with an economy dominated
by its industrial and sophisticated service sectors.

Social indicators highlight the changes wrought by these
changes. The Japanese have the highest life expectancy,
combined with the lowest infant mortality rate, in the
world. Physically, prosperity has increased the average
height and weight of the Japanese. According to UNESCO,
the Japanese have the highest literacy rate in the world – a
reflection of the high proportions of Japanese who gradu-
ate from both high school and university. Despite being one
of the most urbanised, densely populated societies in the
world, and in a state of great social flux, Japan has re-

mained comparatively crime-free. In 1987 the homicide rate in Japan was 15 per cent of that in the United States; rape was 4 per cent and robbery was 0.7 per cent. Compared to England and Wales, Japanese crime rates were 23.6 per cent for murder, 13.5 per cent for rape and 2.2 per cent for serious robbery.

The roots of postwar Japan's phenomenal economic growth lay in developments that took place before 1868, during the Tokugawa period. The system introduced by the shogunate to control their rivals stimulated urbanisation. The peaceful environment created by the Tokugawa spurred economic growth which was founded upon one of most sophisticated and productive agricultural sectors in the pre-modern world. Unusually high levels of literacy contributed decisively to the complex commercial structures that emerged. The *samurai*, facing redundancy in their primary function as warriors, became administrators and developed complex bureaucratic structures and practices which were carried into the post-Tokugawa era.

In 1868 Japan went through a revolution. The Meiji restoration brought down the Tokugawa shogunate and was the prelude to tremendous change. The new regime's overriding priorities were to defend Japan and secure recognition of the nation's equality with the western powers. In the next fifty years Japan's social, economic and political institutions were thoroughly renovated. The rigid social system of Tokugawa Japan was ended. Drawing on models from the west, the armed forces, the legal system and education were transformed. The new government sponsored and encouraged the creation and development of an industrial economy which, by the beginning of the twentieth century, was expanding rapidly. At the centre of this industrial economy were the large, integrated industrial and financial conglomerates, *zaibatsu*, a form of economic organisation that survived, in modified form, to dominate post-war Japan's economy. The First World War gave a tremendous boost to Japan's industrial economy. By 1920 the manufacturing sector was more than 50 per cent larger than it had been in 1914; it was also qualitatively greater since the industrial economy after the First World War was technologically far more advanced than it had been at the beginning of the century. Between 1920 and 1931 Japan suffered a series of economic difficulties but not every sector of industry experienced total gloom. New industries, such as electrical goods manufacturing and aircraft, appeared and others continued to develop new processes and technologies. At the same time management methods and employment techniques emerged which contributed to the continued developed of the technologically advanced industries and survived to assist postwar Japan.

The Meiji government transformed Japan's governmental and political structures. A centralised system of administration was created, staffed by an effective, prestigious and highly influential professional civil service. This bureaucracy would be a powerful element in Japanese government and politics for more than a century. In 1889 the regime promulgated a constitution, based on western models. As a result in 1890 Japan became the first non-western nation to hold a general election for a national parliament. This parliament had not been intended to provide any serious challenge to the government. In fact, it articulated most of the grievances produced by the transformation of Japan after 1870. Groups in the new parliament coalesced to form rudimentary political parties and by 1900 the government was forced to follow suit and organise its own party. Within twenty years Japan had the rudiments of a two-party system. During the 1920s, Japan seemed to become a parliamentary democracy. This era of 'Taishō democracy' rested on flawed foundations. Defects in the political parties and the governments they formed, along with the inability of party governments to solve Japan's domestic and foreign problems, eroded popular support for democracy. Parliamentary democracy was also undermined from without by the powerful bureaucracy and by the military, which was the most potent single institution in prewar Japan. By 1932 the experiment with parliamentary democracy had failed.

After 1931 Japan embarked on a policy of foreign conquest. The prime movers in this policy were the army and, to a lesser extent, the navy. Expansion, however, was supported by significant elements in the bureaucracy, big business and by public opinion. These foreign adventures reflected and reinforced extreme nationalism. The objectives of expansion and conquest changed with time but the search for secure economic resources was a constant factor. This expansionist foreign policy had brought Japan to war with China by 1937 and it produced frequent clashes with the western powers, especially the United States. Tensions between Japan and the United States intensified as the Japanese eyed the resources of south-east Asia. The occupation of the southern part of French Indochina in July 1941 provoked the United States into cutting off Japan's supply of oil. When the Americans refused to relent, the Japanese attacked Pearl Harbor and started the Pacific War. Japan was initially victorious but the inexorable application of superior resources by the United States and its allies ground Japan down. Following a ferocious strategic bombing campaign, and the use of atomic bombs, Japan surrendered on 15 August 1945.

The consequence of defeat was occupation by foreigners. In a variety of ways, the Japanese were fortunate. Since the occupation was an American monopoly it did not threaten national unity and Japan was not divided into different occupied zones as happened to Germany and Korea. The reforms that the occupation authorities imposed made an enormous contribution to the subsequent development of Japan. The new constitution imposed on Japan remains unamended. Radical land reform not only ended previously chronic conflict in rural Japan but also created a class of small-scale peasant landowners who became the basis of conservative dominance of government for twenty years. The remodelled education system was a vital element in dramatically improving the quality of the Japanese workforce, and that quality was one of the fundamental inputs into the postwar economy. In a very real sense, the occupation helped to keep large sections of the population alive.

The United States also provided critical material aid which helped keep the industrial economy ticking over. The beneficial nature of the occupation is clearly shown by the absence of any serious popular resistance to it or to its reforms.

Japan had suffered an intensive strategic bombing campaign but this had wrought rather less physical damage upon Japan's industrial infrastructure than first appearances indicated. None the less, industrial activity was at a virtual standstill by the summer of 1945 and recovery was very slow and patchy. The Korean War, which broke out in 1950, was the first serious stimulus to the postwar economy. By the middle of the 1950s Japan had regained the economic levels it had enjoyed in the mid-1930s. The government and its ministries, principally the Ministry of Finance and the Ministry of International Trade and Industry (MITI) had the means to direct development in significant areas of industry. Symbolically, the beginnings of high-speed growth came with the Income-Doubling Plan in 1960. In reality, it had started before the Plan was proclaimed. Between 1960 and 1973 Japan enjoyed unprecedented levels of growth. Industry changed not only in scale but also in nature. New products were manufactured and marketed. By 1970 Japan had overtaken West Germany and become the second largest economy in the non-communist world.

Japan's period of high-speed growth became popularly known as the 'economic miracle'. So far as is known, miracles do not take place in economic development and the economic transformation of Japan after 1950 had a number of concrete causes. The Japanese enjoyed an unprecedentedly open international economic climate in an age of enormous worldwide economic expansion. The liberal economic environment enabled Japan, a relatively late starter, to import the latest technology without having to meet the full costs of research and development. High levels of investment enabled some Japanese industries to reach and remain at the cutting edge of technology. The GATT trade regime meant that Japan could sell its burgeoning production of manufactured goods with the minimum of restriction, although the domestic market remained the main source of industrial growth. The *keiretsu*, the huge conglomerates, provided relationships between financial institutions and manufacturing industry which facilitated high levels of investment. In Japan, extraordinarily effective methods of management, frameworks for industrial relations and co-operation between the state and private enterprise contributed enormously to the 'miracle'. Entrenched social attitudes and behaviour added to the effectiveness of these structures.

The role of the government and bureaucracy in fostering and directing economic growth remained controversial. In the 1950s MITI and the Ministry of Finance did have the means to influence business decisions significantly. During the period of high-speed growth, and beyond, the formal power of these and other bureaucratic institutions declined. None the less, relations between large-scale business, bureaucracy and government remained unusually close. The 'administrative guidance' delivered to the private sector by MITI and its fellow ministries was never all-powerful, and there were instances of it being ignored. On balance, however, there was usually no significant conflict between the 'guidance' given and the interests of the companies and industries who received it.

High-speed growth ceased in 1973, arrested not only by the first 'oil shock' but also by faulty government policies and, more basically, by Japan reaching the threshold of economies of scale and labour productivity increase through investment and importing technology. After the 1973–4 recession Japan did not again experience growth of more than 6 per cent a year. The economy did recover and weathered the second 'oil shock' of 1979 successfully. The technological sophistication of Japanese manufacturing methods and the goods they produced rapidly advanced. By 1980 Japan was on the way to becoming the world's largest producer of motor vehicles. In the 1980s the domestic economy grew well and seemed able to evade the recession which hit the rest of the industrialised world in the latter part of the decade. Japan's economy also boomed internationally. As Japan's position in the international economy grew, so did criticism from others. Accusations that Japan had achieved the status of economic superpower by unfair practices and discriminatory economic structures led to serious friction, most seriously with the United States, Japan's most important economic and political partner. The demands which the Americans made of Japan produced difficult problems for the Japanese both at home and abroad.

An important ingredient in postwar Japan's economic success was political stability. The same conservative party monopolised government between 1955 and 1993. The Liberal Democratic Party's dominance was in part the result of its political qualities and skill. The party was careful to keep pace with the social changes brought by rapid industrialisation and urbanisation. At critical times, such as after the Security Treaty crisis in 1960 and following the appearance of mass movements protesting against pollution in the late 1960s, the LDP could be remarkably responsive to public moods. The LDP manipulated Japan's unusual electoral system with consummate skill and expertise. The party apparatus and leadership became increasingly adept at generating the vast sums of money required to sustain it in office, although this ultimately was an important factor in the LDP losing its monopoly of office in the summer of 1993. A fundamental component in the LDP dominance of politics was the nature of the opposition. The LDP faced a united political opposition only between 1955 and 1960. In 1960 the main opposition party, the Japan Socialist Party, split. In 1964 the establishment of Kōmeitō, the Buddhist-inspired party, further fragmented the opposition, as did a revival in fortunes of the Japan Communist Party. The opposition remained fatally divided and the LDP lost office in 1993 because of defections from the party, not because of the strategies and tactics of the opposition parties.

Political stability meant consistent government policies,

which helped long-term planning by companies and politicians, bureaucrats and business leaders, who developed close and sustained relationships. There was a price to be paid for this political stability. Monopoly of office and the arrogance of power spawned corruption and scandal. The recipients of much of this illicit funding which washed around conservative politics were the factions. At first, these factions reflected the different conservative parties that had merged to create the LDP. They also mirrored the tensions between career politicians and ex-bureaucrats. These factions seldom represented ideological or political differences. They were the personal followings of leaders, ambitious for office, who could provide funds to fuel the electoral system. These factions, and their leaders, were the centre of 'money politics' which came to dominate the LDP. The Japanese public were unusually tolerant of their politicians' failings until the late 1980s, although scandals frequently ruffled the political fabric.

In the late 1980s the upper reaches of the Japanese politic establishment was savagely pummelled by a wave of revelations of corruption. The reverberations of this buffetting continued as Japan fell into its worst economic downturn since 1950. The old guard in the LDP, the faction leaders, bitterly resisted rising demands for political reform to curb the scandals associated with 'money politics'. Ultimately, this led to defections which ended the party's monopoly of power in August 1993. For the first time for nearly forty years, Japan had a non-LDP government. The seven-party coalition took office at a time of grim economic recession which led commentators to question the effectiveness and survival of some of the basic structures of Japan's postwar economy. Japan, the economic superpower, seems at a significant crossroads.

APPENDIX

JAPANESE PRIME MINISTERS, 1945–94

Higashikuni Naruhiko	17 August 1945–9 October 1945
Shidehara Kijūrō	9 October 1945–22 May 1946
Yoshida Shigeru	22 May 1946–24 May 1947
Katayama Tetsu	24 May 1947–10 March 1948
Ashida Hitoshi	10 March 1948–15 October 1948
Yoshida Shigeru	15 October 1948–10 December 1954
Hatoyama Ichirō	10 December 1954–23 December 1956
Ichibashi Tanzan	23 December 1956–25 February 1957
Kishi Nobusuke	25 February 1957–19 July 1960
Ikeda Hayato	19 July 1960–9 November 1964
Sato Eisaku	9 November 1964–6 July 1972
Tanaka Kakuei	6 July 1972–9 December 1974
Miki Takeo	9 December 1974–24 December 1976
Fukuda Takeo	24 December 1976–7 December 1978
Ōhira Masayoshi	7 December 1978–17 July 1980
Suzuki Zenkō	17 July 1980–27 November 1982
Nakasone Yasuhiro	27 November 1982–6 November 1987
Takeshita Noboru	6 November 1987–2 June 1989
Uno Sousuke	2 June 1989–9 August 1989
Kaifu Toshiki	9 August 1989–5 November 1991
Miyazawa Kiichi	5 November 1991–8 August 1993
Hosokawa Morihiro	8 August 1993–25 April 1994
Hata Tsutomu	25 April 1994–29 June 1994
Murayama Tomiichi	29 June 1994–

BIBLIOGRAPHY

Akita, G., *The Foundations of Constitutional Government in Japan 1868–1900* (Cambridge, Mass., 1969).

Aoki, Masahiko, 'The Japanese Firm in Transition', in Kozo Yamamura and Yasukich Yasuba (eds), *The Political Economy of Japan*, vol. 1, *The Domestic Transformation* (Stanford, Calif., 1987).

Baerwald, Hans H., *The Purge of Japanese Leaders under the Occupation* (Berkeley, Calif., 1959).

Baerwald, Hans J., *Party Politics in Japan* (London, 1986).

Baerwald, Hans H., 'Early SCAP Policy and the Rehabilitation of the Diet', in Robert E. Ward and Sakamoto Yoshikazu (eds), *Democratizing Japan: The Allied Occupation* (Honolulu, 1987).

Barnhart, Michael, *Japan Prepares for Total War: The Search for Economic Security 1919–1941* (Ithaca, NY and London, 1987).

Beasley, W. G., *Japanese Imperialism 1894–1945* (Oxford, 1987).

Beasley, W. G., *The Rise of Modern Japan* (London, 1990).

Berton, Peter, 'The Japan Communist Party: The "Lovable" Party', R. J. Hrebenar *et al.* (eds), *The Japanese Party System: From One-Party Rule to Coalition Government* (Boulder, Colo. and London, 1986).

Boltho, Andrea, *Japan: An Economic Survey 1953–1973* (London, 1975).

Butow, Robert J. C., *Tojo and the Coming of the War* (Stanford, Calif. 1961).

Calder, Kent E., *Crisis and Compensation: Public Policy and Political Stability in Japan, 1949–1986* (Princeton, NJ, 1988).

Caves, Richard E., 'Industrial Organization', in H. Patrick and

H. Rosovsky (eds), *Asia's New Giant: How the Japanese Economy Works* (Washington, DC, 1976).

Caves, Richard E. and Uekusa, M., *Industrial Organization in Japan* (Washington, DC, 1976).

Curtis, Gerald L., *The Japanese Way of Politics* (New York, 1988).

Denison, E. F. and Chung, W. K., 'Economic Growth and its Sources', in H. Patrick and H. Rosovsky (eds), *Asia's New Giant: How the Japanese Economy Works* (Washington, DC, 1976).

Dore, Ronald, *Land Reform in Japan* (London, 1959).

Dore, Ronald, *British Factory–Japanese Factory: The Origins of National Diversity in Industrial Relations* (Berkeley and Los Angeles, Calif., 1973).

Dower, J. W., *Empire and Aftermath: Yoshida Shigeru and the Japanese Experience, 1878–1954* (Cambridge, Mass. and London, 1979).

Duus, Peter, *Party Rivalry and Political Change in Taishō Japan* (Cambridge, Mass. and London, 1968).

Eades, George C. and Yamamura, Kozo, 'The Future of Industrial Policy', in Kozo Yamamura and Yasukich Yasuba (eds), *The Political Economy of Japan*, vol. 1, *The Domestic Transformation* (Stanford, Calif., 1987).

Emmerson, J. K., *Arms, Yen and Power: The Japanese Dilemma* (New York, 1971).

Emmott, Bill, *The Sun Also Sets: Why Japan Will Not Be Number One* (London and New York, 1989).

Emmott, Bill, *Japan's Global Reach* (London, 1993).

Finn, Richard B., *Winners in Peace: MacArthur, Yoshida and Postwar Japan* (Berkeley and Los Angeles, Calif., 1992).

Francks, Penelope, *Japanese Economic Development: Theory and Practice* (London, 1992).

Fransman, Martin, *The Market and Beyond: Information Technology in Japan* (Cambridge, 1990).

Fruin, W. Mark, *The Japanese Enterprise System: Competitive Strategies and Cooperative Structures* (Oxford, 1992).

Fukui, Haruhiro, 'Postwar Politics, 1945–1973', in Peter Duus (ed.), *The Cambridge History of Japan*, vol. 6 (1988).

Fukutake, Tadashi, *The Japanese Social Structure: Its Evolution in the Modern Century* (Tokyo, 1982).

Garon, Sheldon, *The State and Labor in Modern Japan* (Berkeley and Los Angeles, Calif., 1987).

Gordon, Andrew, 'Contests for the Workplace', in Andrew Gordon (ed.), *Postwar Japan as History* (Berkeley, Calif., 1993).

Hadley, Eleanor M., *Antitrust in Japan* (Princeton, NJ, 1970).

Harries, Meirion and Harries, Susie, *Sheathing the Sword: The Demilitarisation of Japan* (London, 1987).

Havens, Thomas R. H., *Fire Across the Sea: The Vietnam War and Japan 1965–1975* (Princeton, NJ, 1987).

Hayami, Yujiro, *Japanese Agriculture Under Siege: The Political Economy of Agricultural Policies* (London, 1988).

Hayao, Kenji, *The Japanese Prime Minister and Public Policy* (Pittsburgh, Penn., 1993).

Hayes, Louis D., *Introduction to Japanese Politics* (New York, 1992).

Herzog, Peter J., *Japan's Pseudo-Democracy* (Folkestone, 1993).

Hirschmeier J. and Yui, T., *The Development of Japanese Business*, 2nd edn (London, 1981).

Horioka, Charles Y., 'Consuming and Saving', in Andrew Gordon (ed.), *Postwar Japan as History* (Berkeley, Calif., 1993).

Horsley, William and Buckley, Roger, *Nippon: New Superpower. Japan since 1945* (London, 1990).

Hrebenar, Ronald J., 'The Kōmeitō: Party of "Buddhist Democracy"', in R. J. Hrebenar *et al.*, *The Japanese Party System* (1986a).

Hrebenar, Ronald J., 'The Money Base of Japanese Politics', in R. J. Hrebenar *et al.*, *The Japanese Party System* (1986b).

Hrebenar, Ronald J. *et al.* (eds), *The Japanese Party System: From One-Party Rule to Coalition Government* (Boulder, Colo. and London, 1986).

Hunter, Janet E., *The Emergence of Modern Japan: An Introductory History since 1853* (London, 1989).

Ike, Nobutake, *Japan's Decision for War: Records of the 1941 Policy Conferences* (Stanford, Calif., 1967).

Inoguchi, Takashi and Okimoto, Daniel I. (eds), *The Political Economy of Japan*, vol. 2, *The Changing International Context* (1988).

Iriye, Akira, *The Origins of the Second World War in Asia and the Pacific* (London and New York, 1987).

Ishihara, Shintaro, *The Japan That Can Say No* (London 1991); originally published in 1989 as *'No' to Ieru Nihon*.

Ito, Takatoshi, *The Japanese Economy* (Cambridge, Mass. and London, 1992).

Johnson, Chalmers, *MITI and the Japanese Miracle* (Stanford, Calif., 1986).

Kawai, Kazuo, *Japan's American Interlude* (Chicago, Ill. London, 1960).

Komiya, Ryutaro, Okuno, Masahiro and Suzumura, Kotaro (eds), *Industrial Policy of Japan* (Tokyo, 1988).

Kosai, Yutaka, *The Era of High-Speed Growth: Notes on the Postwar Japanese Economy* (Tokyo, 1986).

Kosai, Yutaka, 'The Postwar Japanese Economy, 1945–1975', in Peter Duus (ed.), *The Cambridge History of Japan*, vol. 6 (1988).

Kosaka, Masataka, *A History of Postwar Japan* (Tokyo, 1972).

Kumon, Shumpei and Rosovsky, Henry, *The Political Economy of Japan*, vol. 3, *Cultural and Social Dynamics* (1992).

Kurzman, Dan, *Kishi and Japan: The Search for the Sun* (New York, 1960).

Large, Stephen S., *Emperor Hirohito and Showa Japan: A Political Biography* (London, 1992).

Lehmann, Jean-Pierre, *The Roots of Modern Japan* (London, 1982).

Lincoln, Edward J., *Japan: Facing Economic Maturity* (Washington, DC, 1988).

McMillan, Charles J., *The Japanese Industrial System*, 2nd rev. edn (Berlin and New York, 1985).

McNelly, Theodore H., '"Induced Revolution": The Policy of Process of Constitutional Reform in Occupied Japan', in Robert E. Ward and Sakamoto Yoshikazu (eds), *Democratizing Japan: The Allied Occupation* (Honolulul, 1987).

MacPherson, W. J., *The Economic Development of Japan c. 1868–1941* (London, 1987).

Minami, Royshin, *The Economic Development of Japan: A Quantitative Study* (London, 1986).

Moore, Joe, *Japanese Workers and the Struggle for Power 1945–1947* (Madison, Wis., 1983).

Morishima, Michio, *Why Has Japan 'Succeeded'?* (London, 1982).

Morley, James W. (ed.), *Dilemmas of Growth in Prewar Japan* (Princeton, NJ, 1971).

Murakami, Yasusuke, 'The Japanese Model of Political Economy', in Kozo Yamamura and Yasukich Yasuba (eds), *The Political Economy of Japan*, vol. 1, *The Domestic Transformation* (Stanford, Calif., 1987).

Mutoh, Hiromichi, 'The Automotive Industry', in Ryutaro Komiya, Masahiro Okuno and Kotaro Suzumura (eds), *Industrial Policy in Japan* (Tokyo, 1988).

Nakamura, Takafusa, *The Postwar Japanese Economy: Its Development and Structure* (Tokyo, 1981).

Nakamura, Takafusa, *Economic Growth in Prewar Japan* (New Haven, Conn. and London, 1983).

Nakamura, Takafusa, 'The Japanese Economy in the Interwar Period: a Brief Summary', in Ronald Dore and Radha Sinha (eds), *Japan and World Depression: Then and Now* (London, 1987).

Nester, William R., *The Foundations of Japanese Power: Continuities, Changes, Challenges* (London, 1990).

Okimoto, Daniel, *Between MITI and the Market: Japanese Industrial Policy for High Technology* (Stanford, Calif., 1989).

Oppler, Alfred C., *Legal Reform in Occupied Japan* (Princeton, NJ, 1976).

Piccigallo, Philip R., *The Japanese on Trial: Allied War Crimes Operations in the East, 1945–1951* (Austin, Tex. and London, 1979).

Passin, Herbert, *Society and Education in Japan* (New York, 1965).

Passin, Herbert, *Encounter with Japan* (New York and Tokyo, 1982).

Patrick, Hugh T., 'The Economic Muddle of the 1920's', in James W. Morley (ed.), *Dilemmas of Growth in Prewar Japan* (Princeton, NJ, 1971).

Patrick, Hugh and Rosovsky, Henry, *Asia's New Giant: How the Japanese Economy Works* (Washington, DC, 1976).

Patrick, Hugh and Rosovsky, Henry, 'Japan's Economic Performance: An Overview', in H. Patrick and H. Rosovsky (eds), *Asia's New Giant: How the Japanese Economy Works* (Washington, DC, 1976).

Peck, Merton and Tamura, Shuji, 'Technology', in H. Patrick and H. Rosovsky (eds), *Asia's New Giant: How the Japanese Economy Works* (Washington, DC, 1976).

Reading, Brian, *Japan: The Coming Collapse* (London, 1992).

Richardson, Bradly M. and Flanagan, Scott C., *Politics in Japan* (Boston, Mass., 1984).

Roberts, John G., *Mitsui* (New York, 1973).

Rohlen, Thomas P., 'Learning: The Mobilization of Knowledge in the Japanese Political Economy', in Shumpei Kumon and Henry Rosovsky (eds), *The Political Economy of Japan*, vol. 3, *Cultural and Social Dynamics* (1992).

Scalapino, Robert A., *Democracy and the Party Movement in Prewar Japan* (Berkeley and Los Angeles, Calif., 1962).

Schaller, Michael, *The American Occupation of Japan: The Origins of the Cold War in Asia* (Oxford and New York, 1985).

Schaller, Michael, *Douglas MacArthur: The Far Eastern General* (Oxford, 1989).

Shillony, Ben-Ami, *Politics and Culture in Wartime Japan* (Oxford, 1981).

Shimada, Haruo, 'Japan's Industrial Culture and Labor–Management Relations', in S. Kumon and P. Rosovsky (eds), *The Political Economy of Japan*, vol. 2, *Cultural and Social Dynamics* (1992).

Sigal, Leon V., *Fighting to a Finish: The Politics of War Termination in the United States and Japan, 1945* (Ithaca, NY, 1988).

Spaulding, Robert M., Jr, 'The Bureaucracy as a Political Force, 1920–45', in James W. Morley (ed.), *Dilemmas of Growth in Prewar Japan* (Princeton, NJ, 1971).

Spector, Ronald E., *Eagle Against the Sun: The American War with Japan* (London and New York, 1984).

Stockwin, J. A. A., *Japan: Divided Politics in a Growth Economy* (London, 1982).

Stockwin, J. A. A., 'The Japan Socialist Party: A Politics of Permanent Opposition', in R. J. Hrebenar *et al.* (eds), *The Japanese Party System: From One-Party Rule to Coalition Government* (Boulder, Colo. and London, 1986).

Stockwin, J. A. A. 'Parties, Politicians and the Political System', in J. A. A. Stockwin (ed.), *Dynamic and Immobilist Politics in Japan* (Basingstoke, 1988).

Suzuki, Yoshitaka, *Japanese Management Structures 1920–80* (London, 1991).

Teidemann, Arthur E., 'Big Business and Politics in Prewar Japan', in James W. Morley (ed.), *Dilemmas of Growth in Prewar Japan* (Princeton, NJ, 1971).

Thayer, Nathaniel, *How the Conservatives Rule Japan* (Princeton, NJ, 1969).

Tomita Nobuo, Nakamura, Akira and Ronald J. Hrebenar, 'The Liberal Democratic Party: The Ruling Party of Japan', in R. J. Hrebenar *et al.* (eds), *The Japanese Party System: From One-Party Rule to Coalition Government* (Boulder, Colo. and London, 1986).

Tresize, Philip H. and Suzuki, Yukio, 'Politics, Government and Economic Growth in Japan', in H. Patrick and H. Rosovsky (eds), *Asia's New Giant: How the Japanese Economy Works* (Washington, DC, 1976).

Tsuru, Shigeto, *Japan's Capitalism: Creative Defeat and Beyond* (Cambridge, 1993).

Uchino, Tatsuro, *Japan's Postwar Economy: An Insider's View of its History and its Future* (Tokyo, 1983).

Uekusa, Masu, 'The Oil Crisis and After', in Ryutaro Komiya, Masahiro Okuno and Kotaro Suzumaura (eds), *Industrial Policy in Japan* (Tokyo, 1988).

Ward, Robert E. and Sakamoto Yoshikazu (ed.), *Democratizing Japan: The Allied Occupation* (Honolulu, 1987).

Ward, Robert E., 'Presurrender Planning: Treatment of the Emperor and Constitutional Changes', in Robert E. Ward and Sakamoto Yoshikazu (eds), *Democratizing Japan: The Allied Occupation* (Honolulu, 1987).

White, James W., 'The Dynamics of Political Opposition', in Andrew Gordon (ed.), *Postwar Japan as History* (Berkeley, Calif., 1993).

Wood, Christopher, *The Bubble Economy: The Japanese Economic Collapse* (Tokyo, 1992).

Woronoff, Jon, *Politics the Japanese Way* (London, 1986).

Yamamura, Kozo and Yasuba, Yasukichi (eds), *The Political Economy of Japan*, vol. 1, *The Domestic Transformation* (Stanford, Calif., 1987).

INDEX